AUTOBIOGRAHY OF A
FREEDOM
RIDER

My Life as a Foot Soldier
for Civil Rights

Thomas M. Armstrong and Natalie R. Bell

Health Communications, Inc.
Deerfield Beach, Florida

www.hcibooks.com

For Jeanette,

Aleena,

Kimberly, and Cynthia

Library of Congress Cataloging-in-Publication Data

Armstrong, Thomas M., 1941–
Autobiography of a freedom rider : my life as a foot soldier for civil rights /
  Thomas M. Armstrong and Natalie R. Bell.
      p. cm.
    Includes bibliographical references.
    ISBN-13: 978-0-7573-1603-6 (trade paper)
    ISBN-10: 0-7573-1603-4 (trade paper)
    ISBN-13: 978-0-7573-9171-2 (e-book)
    ISBN-10: 0-7573-9171-0 (e-book)
1. Armstrong, Thomas M., 1941– 2. Civil rights movements—Mississippi—
  History—20th century. 3. African Americans—Civil rights Mississippi—
  History—20th century. 4. Freedom Rides, 1961. 5. Civil rights workers—
  Mississippi—Biography. 6. African American civil rights workers—Mississippi—
  Biography. 7. Mississippi—Race relations—History—20th century.
  I. Bell, Natalie R. II. Title.
  E185.93.M6A76 2011
  323.092--dc22
  [B]

                                                                    2011013920

Publisher: Health Communications, Inc.
        3201 S.W. 15th Street
        Deerfield Beach, FL 33442–8190

Cover image ©Getty Images
Cover design by Larissa Hise Henoch
Interior design and formatting by Lawna Patterson Oldfield

Contents

∞

Part Two: Answering the Call

Part Three: Remembering the Call

Foreword

⸚⸚⸚

THOMAS ARMSTRONG'S DECISION to join the 1961 Freedom Rides secured his place in history as the first Mississippian to do so. His commitment to make a difference and speak out against injustice was reinforced by his experiences as a student at Tougaloo College, where the significance of education to promote transformative change is so well evidenced. An oasis of freedom and intellectual ideals, Tougaloo College continues to prepare its students for lives of meaning and to use their education to effect change in a global economy.

Known as the "Cradle of the Civil Rights Movement in Mississippi," Tougaloo College is the place to which people from across

America came to devise the strategies to improve race relations in Mississippi. The college became—without regard to race, ethnicity, gender, or religion—the safe haven and refuge from the raging storm of racism that permeated the state of Mississippi during that period in history. From the sanctuary of its Woodworth Chapel, strategies were devised to change the social, political, and economic fibers of the state of Mississippi; strategies that would ultimately impact the nation, creating a model for those fighting for democracy worldwide. Such was the influence of a Tougaloo education for the students of that time who were charged with the responsibility to make a difference. From the Tougaloo Nine to the Freedom Riders, the civil rights movement was significantly influenced by the young peoples' engagement.

The youth of today is not much different from those of yesteryear. They want to believe that their generation can also make a difference and are inspired to do so. They, too, are seeking opportunities to grab onto a cause bigger than themselves. Young people became engaged in helping the victims of Hurricane Katrina: they flocked to New Orleans and the Mississippi Gulf Coast to volunteer at the shelters and to assist with the rebuilding efforts. They became engaged in the presidential campaign of President Barack Obama and voted in record numbers for change. They realized that their votes mattered and they could make a difference.

The lessons of the past must be shared with young people today, to enable them to understand conceptually and contextually the difference each succeeding generation can make, and their responsibility to advance the ideals of a democratic society. Thomas Armstrong's story will inspire them to find their places of impact and influence.

There are valuable lessons to glean from Thomas Armstrong's life as a Freedom Rider and foot soldier for justice and equality. His journey is an example of students' social activism and how it influenced a movement that broke through the walls of segregation, destroyed the barriers of Jim Crow, and gave wings to a movement that resulted in African Americans' rise to full citizenship in the Deep South under the law.

While the highly emotionally charged civil rights era has passed, there are indeed important lessons that are instructive for educators and students today. Along with uncompromising academic preparation, students must also prepared to meet the challenges of informed citizenship, to be sensitive and committed to the issues of justice, and to develop the quality of character that is essential for productive participation in the global society. Autobiography of a Freedom Rider will help encourage and inspire the next generation to continue constructing the path toward a true and inclusive democracy.

Beverly Wade Hogan
President, Tougaloo College

Introduction

∽

I MARVEL AT THE WAY THE American civil rights movement
continually inspires people all over the world, and how the Freedom Rides of 1961 are seen as a key accelerant in the movement
that opened the way to revolutionary change in this nation.

Long before anyone dreamed that racial integration was possible
in the South or anywhere blacks were excluded, interracial teams
of Americans boarded Greyhound and Trailways buses, as well as
other modes of interstate travel, and rode fearlessly into the segregated South. In addition to a series of bus rides, the Freedom Rides
included other dramatic demonstrations, constituting a pivotal
moment in American history.

The range of reactions in the South varied from town to town, and the roles of Southerners were often quite different from what has been written in historical accounts. Many of us born and raised in the Jim Crow South were transformed by the power of nonviolent direct action, and moved to confront the laws and customs under which we had been formed. The Freedom Riders were themselves a diverse group of individuals from all over the country.

Hardly anyone today, it seems, realizes the terror that existed among black Southerners during most of the last century, and that a generation of Americans who experienced that life remain very much a part of contemporary society. Fannie Lou Hamer once described precisely what it was like: "There's so much hate. Only God has kept the Negro sane."

Those who branched out into that sea of hate, especially those of us who formed the basis of the Student Nonviolent Coordinating Committee (SNCC) in Mississippi, were labeled as misfits and agitators by mainstream society in the early 1960s. It took tremendous courage for us to stand up to the violence of the Ku Klux Klan and the White Citizens' Council; and yet, as responsible citizens, we would not be deterred from striving for justice, truly one of the noblest goals any of us can strive for.

The early days of the civil rights movement were among the most important of my life. My movement friends and I formed a bond of intense love for each other like I have not felt since my participation in the movement, which lasted from 1958 to 1963. This frequently misunderstood period of history helped propel the larger movement that followed, and acknowledgment must be given to various events that had been quietly playing out for at least a decade prior to my involvement.

Most people were not inclined to take the risk we did: to break the code of conduct that divided the South into separate worlds. By railing against what was then the norm, we placed ourselves in harm's way through nonviolent means. As a consequence, I was forced, against my will, to sever ties with my parents and others in my extended family in the all-black community of Lucas in South Mississippi.

The 1960s' fight for freedom in America was not unlike our 1930s' Abraham Lincoln Brigade in the Spanish Civil War, or the organization of industrial workers in the CIO, or our fight against fascism in World War II. But unlike veterans of each of those struggles, our hurt veterans had no post-struggle support system. There was no "Veterans of the Lincoln Brigade" organization, no labor unions to provide emotional and financial support for its early organizers, no GI Bill to provide financial aid, or Veterans Administration to provide physical and mental-health care.

Some of us walked through those times physically unscarred, and yet we experienced deep and intense fear. We became the walking wounded, suffering from the dramatic effects of post-traumatic stress syndrome. In many cases, this manifested into addictions of various kinds, homelessness, mental illness and other problems. Most of us are forever altered from our civil rights experiences.

For nearly forty years, I seldom talked about my engagement in the movement, an era that represented one of the most restrictive environments for a person of color in Mississippi's history. I had placed those days far back in my mind, although I never regretted the choice I made to proclaim publicly that segregation was wrong. However, in recent years, I've become concerned that succeeding generations may never fully recognize the magnitude of sacrifice that tens of thousands of people—the foot soldiers—gave in the civil rights movement in the name of a true and inclusive democracy.

I began to revisit this period of my life about ten years ago, when the classified files of the now defunct Mississippi State Sovereignty Commission were made public. I was finally able to see some of what I had suspected over the years but could only imagine. The files contained evidence that I, and many others I knew, had been spied upon by fellow citizens during that time.

Created two years after the 1954 Supreme Court ruling on Brown v. Board of Education, which declared racially segregated schools unconstitutional, the Sovereignty Commission's stated mission was to "protect the sovereignty of the state of Mississippi and her sister states" from federal government interference.

The Commission officially closed in 1977. Legal challenges over privacy issues delayed release of its files until 1998. The files are now available through the Mississippi State Department of Archives and History, which has created an online database, accessible from its website.

Among many revelations in the files is the fact that the Commission collaborated with the notorious White Citizens' Councils to spy on civil rights workers. This memoir exposes the findings of the Commission's investigations that focused on me and people I knew.

During the years 1960–1964, the Sovereignty Commission spent a tremendous amount of energy investigating me. The state-funded agency sent investigators into my home community to interview some of my teachers, friends, and relatives. During each encounter, the investigators would tell the interviewee not to tell anyone what was asked or said. Of course, after the interviews, many of these people reported directly to my family. Each of them said they provided very little information to the investigators. Many stated that they didn't know my family, or that I may have been a member of other Armstrong families who lived near my home near Prentiss, Mississippi. This was a way of local blacks taking care of their own.

I want to make note of the fact that Mississippi, the heart of Southern tradition, is a far different place today than it was in the 1960s. As Jan Hillegas, one of my friends who helped open the door to change and still lives in the state, likes to say, it is a "New Mississippi."

A flowering of the black middle class and political influence in the state point to major improvements that can be directly linked to the end of segregation, which came to pass less than fifty years ago.

Much of the South has entered an era of reconciliation with its divided past. Mississippi is taking steps to commission a Civil Rights Museum and a string of Civil Rights Heritage sites. My former high school, Prentiss Normal and Industrial Institute, one of a handful open to blacks when I was growing up, has been designated a state historical landmark.

The sheer depth of change we managed to make with our weapons of moral and spiritual forces left me breathless when I returned to Mississippi in 2001 for the fortieth anniversary of the Freedom Rides. It was the first time I had been there with Joan Trumpauer Mulholland since the 1960s, when it was dangerous for me to be seen in public with her because we are of different skin color. When we were college students working as organizers in the Freedom Movement, we would sometimes drive into Jackson, and Joan would have to lie down on the rear seat so as not to be seen by other whites. Riding in the car with her through the streets of Jackson now was very strange, and strangely wonderful, indeed. The following year, an extended drive through rural North Mississippi with Dorie Ladner and Jan Hillegas, who is also Caucasian, produced that same feeling. We traveled to Philadelphia for a program honoring the lives of James Chaney, Andrew Goodman, and Michael Schwerner.

The election of President Barack Obama was the culmination of the efforts of thousands of people, just like me, who realized the need to create a more-perfect union. Some of those people, those foot soldiers, died in their quest to make such an election possible. Now each of us shares the responsibility to go a step further, to make this great country even greater.

There is a new movement afoot, led by a new generation of young people, that is not aimed at fighting *against* injustice, but *for the creation of equality and justice for all people*. This important job requires us to think beyond ourselves and work for the betterment of others. That is how the Freedom Riders seized the attention of the nation in 1961. When ordinary men and women saw that progress was possible, and despite often violent opposition, they wasted no time in taking action; they made a difference.

Whatever difference I might have made, the civil rights movement has given me much in return: a true sense of purpose and an abiding personal fulfillment.

Thomas M. Armstrong

Part One:

Receiving
the Call

1

⧓

Opportunity Denied

A S A YOUNG MAN GROWING UP in the 1950s in an all-black community called Lucas, my home deep in the Piney Woods of southern Mississippi, I would often stay awake until a quarter past ten to listen to the Blues on the radio. Jimmy Reed, Muddy Waters, and Little Junior Parker were some of my favorite artists (and I can't leave out Howling Wolf, Etta James, and Chuck Berry). Oh yes. The Blues could make whatever was going wrong feel all right. I had to sneak the old Philco radio under the bedcovers, so Dad would not hear it. He didn't like the Blues, and took every advantage of his ability to tell me, "Boy, turn that thing off." As far as Dad was concerned, the Blues was "devil's" music. He felt the same way about dancing and playing cards. More to his liking were the songs we sang at church, or the country quartet singing that was common around my home. People would get together with family and friends and harmonize for entertainment, singing to the likes of the Five Blind Boys of Mississippi, Albertina Walker, and the Spiritual Jubilees. Whether anyone was ready or not, the Blues had come to stay. Lucas had two juke joints, which were the destination for miles around for dancing and socializing on Saturday nights. The clubs could operate in our unincorporated community, because there were no laws to prohibit them, but the local church folks didn't want them there. Fights were known to break out. Occasionally, we'd hear of a shooting or someone knifed in the back. I was too young to get in, but even if I wasn't, these were not the kinds of places I was in the habit of going.

We were situated far from the Mississippi Delta, in the southern half of the state. Agriculture was the major source of income, and the earliest sound of the Blues I remember was from people singing in the fields, which covered the landscape, while they were picking or chopping cotton.

The rhythm of those work songs was not unlike some of the songs we sang at church. Only the words were different: one spoke your feelings about God, another about relationships, how your girl done you wrong, your job, hardships. Some of the church fathers would be tapping their feet, listening to the radio on Saturday mornings, not realizing it was playing the Blues.

I liked country music, too. Blues and country, that's all we had. As we moved about the house on weekends, we'd turn up the volume and listen for the sales pitches for live baby chicks and Royal Crown hairdressing. We grew our own supply of chicks, and a cup of Royal Crown could always be found in the house somewhere. By the time I turned eleven on August 17, 1952, both of my birth parents, Mildred and Thomas Armstrong Jr., had succumbed to separate episodes of illness. My mother died when I was two. My eight siblings and I (six girls, two boys) were split up and taken in by three different families of relatives. By then, I was the youngest. My mother had given birth to another child after me, but he preceded her in death. Prior to her passing, my mother had arranged for my father's sister, Vaudra Armstrong, and her husband, Enoch Barnes, to raise me. They became my legal guardians. When I speak of Mom and Dad, of my parents, I'm speaking of them. Their daughter Nellie, ten years older than I, became my sister.

Once, I overheard a relative ask Enoch and Vaudra why didn't they adopt me and give me their surname. Enoch replied that there was no need to, because he wanted me to always remember my real parents.

Dad didn't have a chance to get an education beyond fourth

grade. Most of his black male peers faced similar circumstances. He had to stop attending school to help support the family. He and his father worked for white people in the logging trade. Determined not to need to depend on anyone to earn a living for himself, Enoch used his knowledge of logging to start his own business. Along with agriculture, forestry was a major industry; thus, he was able to find work most of the year.

He owned several trucks that he used in his business, which was based at the house. I learned to spell the word "Chevrolet" from the side of a 1942 five-ton log truck. Enoch's brother, Clark Barnes, operated a pulpwood business. The two of them, along with brothers Elijah, Nemirah, and Oliver, purchased standing timberland, and, from the sale of logs and pulpwood, they all made a good living. There was another brother, Javis, who chose to live in New Orleans, having declared his dislike for the same logging and farming businesses his siblings naturally gravitated to.

Dad had a regular crew of workers. Most mornings, they would come knocking at the door looking for him, if not to work, then to seek a job. Most of them lived in the community. If they were coming from further away, he might let them board for a time at the house.

Our home was in the countryside, where family status was defined by land ownership, and communities by religion and cultural restraint. Black landowners were not uncommon in the mostly white-populated counties south of Jackson, the state capital, in central Mississippi. Most were farmers. They raised cotton, corn, and other vegetables, and typically worked side-by-side in the fields with their sharecroppers, or hired day laborers. I lived the life of a farm boy on an eighty-acre farm. Most of the food we raised, however, was for the cattle and horses my dad used in his business.

I broke my left arm when I was twelve, the result of an awkward fall: I was trying to jump a fence while training for track. My arm was broken in three places, a disaster that required multiple surgeries, metal screws, and plates. It was left permanently scarred. So, I stopped wearing short-sleeve shirts and kept holding my head high. To my youthful, naïve thinking, life seemed fair—as fair as a segregated state would allow.

Communities like ours, a mix of farmers, skilled tradesmen, and teachers, were proudly self-sufficient. We had our own gristmill, which was open for use by all, for making meal from corn. During most of the Jim Crow era, the Illinois Central Gulf Railroad ran tracks through the community. We had a postmaster who doubled as a stationmaster, and he could be relied upon to find colored folks a decent place to sleep for the night.

As was legal and therefore customary under segregation, blacks were excluded—and often exploited—socially, politically, and economically. Anyway, my parents, like most of their peers, shielded us youngsters from the degradation of this reality. They knew that we would be certain to find out eventually, but like all loving parents, wanted to protect us from the pain of suffering for as long as they could.

Under the race-restrictive laws of the Jim Crow South, few Negroes could find jobs in the industries that began opening in the late 1940s. In the early 1950s in Mississippi, two-thirds were still working in some form of agriculture (by then in economic decline), and the vast majority, 80 percent, were sharecroppers and day laborers. If most of us were poor, we didn't know it; we were not poor in spirit. Most people raised their own food and made many of the products they used. If there was a soul in need, someone could be relied upon to help. Most important, land ownership fueled our drive for better educational and political opportunities. Landowner families were usually able to send their children to school and for longer periods of time, which meant that their descendants most often became teachers and small-business owners.

Lucas, a community of about 100 people, was home to several black land-owning families, whose names included the Halls, Warners, Suttons, Grays, Prices, and my paternal ancestors, the Armstrongs. Each of these families owned an average of two or three hundred acres, land their ancestors had managed to hold onto through a reign of terror by white supremacists in the late nineteenth century. It was a counterrevolution that brought an end to Reconstruction and shattered many of the gains black Mississippians had made after the Civil War.

Lucas had been settled in 1870 by first-generation freedmen who were followers of one Ira Warren Lucas, a black man with relatively substantial means. It is situated in Jefferson Davis County, which was formed in 1906 from two neighboring counties and named for the former president of the Confederacy. The county's population has historically tilted toward a slight black majority.

My parents were the descendants of enslaved grandparents who, after Emancipation, made significant strides on all levels of society, only to see those gains and opportunities later vanish. The black freedmen in Mississippi outnumbered whites, more so than in any other Deep South state. During Reconstruction, many served with distinction in elected offices ranging from constable to United States Senator.

Despite those successes, hundreds of innocent blacks were killed in violent attacks by mobs of white vigilantes bent on returning the state to white supremacist rule beginning in the 1880s. Violence and electoral fraud effectively denied black Mississippians their political rights. It was the start of the Jim Crow era. By 1890, the state had adopted restrictions on voter participation requiring applicants to "read" a section of the state constitution. Before the turn of the century, the legal basis for separate but equal public facilities would be established.

My great-grandparents, Ransom and Caroline Armstrong, who had been able to vote and acquire land during Reconstruction, lived in a constant state of fear in the latter stages of their lives. Six-hundred blacks are on record as having been lynched over the six decades following the 1880s. During the twelve years between 1894 and 1906, at least fourteen lynchings occurred within a 100-mile radius of my ancestral home, according to *Where Rebels Roost* by Susan Klopfer. A black man by the name of Wood Ambrose was lynched in Prentiss on June 11, 1906. Other lynchings occurred over the years in nearby Brookhaven, Hattiesburg and Hazelhurst, and as late as 1930 and 1942 in Scooba and Laurel, respectively.

While I would often hear stories about mistreatment of Negroes, I had never completely felt the indignity of segregation until my second year in high school. My first real-life experience made me realize something wasn't right about the conditions of black folks in Mississippi and helped me understand what that something meant.

From the start, nothing was going right that day, late in the summer of 1954. The memory is so etched into my brain and my bones, I can recall it happening as if it were just this morning.

It's a Friday, and I didn't awaken at the proper time because I had been up late the night before listening to Randy's Records Highlights, the radio broadcast on WLAC out of Nashville, Tennessee. At 7:30 AM, I head out of the house on foot, and because I've missed the bus to school, I'm walking quickly east along the stretch of U.S. Highway 84 that passes through the middle of Lucas.

The highway, originally an Indian Trail that aided early settlers from the East, is a major throughway to Texas. Already, the tropical sun beams down oppressively upon me as I make my way to the local Ball's Grocery. From there, I'll surely find someone to catch a ride with to Prentiss, the largest business district in our area, five miles further east along the highway. Classes will be starting in minutes at Prentiss Normal and Industrial Institute, the private high school and junior college for blacks, located just north of town.

On my way to hitch a ride at Ball's, I pass Cousin Bertha working in her yard. "Hello there," she yells, staring at me with her hand on her hip. I'm sure she knows I'm late for school, but doesn't ask. "Morning," I call back and nod. The thought occurs to me that she's always working in that yard and must have too much time on her hands. Only she and her granddaughter, Catherine, live in the twelve-room home, left to her by her late father.

The early birds are assembling at the store, purchasing fuel for their cars and trucks and getting their supply of cheese and crackers to carry them through the day.

Running now to catch Mr. Arthur Kelly before he pulls away, I slow down and call for him to wait just long enough for me to retrieve pages of homework that had slipped out of my bag and scattered along the highway. Mr. Kelly gives me a sermon that could have been entitled, "Go to sleep early and wake up early." That's the cost of the ride, I decide, once he finally tells me to get in, and he drives the five miles into town. The main street through Prentiss,

State Highway 13, Columbia Avenue as it's known locally, is lined with various shops and small businesses, drugstores, eateries, the Piggly Wiggly, doctors' and lawyers' offices. Before we get to the main strip, he lets me out across from the Dairy King ice-cream shop.

It's early, but already a hot summer day and not too soon for an ice cream cone. I walk up to the front window and place my order. Immediately, I am told I am at the "wrong" window.

"Can't you see the sign?" The attendant jerks his thumb to the side window. As I back away, the large "White Only" sign glares down at me. I walk around to the side window, where a sign on the wall reads, "Colored." Next to it, a large, metal drum used for garbage. It is not covered. A swarm of flies buzzes. I turn to leave the place, letting the flies feast undisturbed, and not waiting for my order to be filled.

So it was, my first, independent meeting with Jim Crow.

The agitated attendant's attitude, as if I had taken something from him, had shocked me. I can still hear the loud command, "Move around to the side window." I had stepped out of my "place." From that day forward I began to hate all white people. Mother would quickly take care of that problem, though, by reminding me that my grandmother, who I knew little about, was white.

Of course, before the ice cream incident, I understood that there were rules that gave whites the advantage over blacks. Most weekends, I would go with my dad into some of the white-owned stores just outside Lucas, where we had to wait until the cashiers finished with all the white people before they took our money.

On this day, however, I had ventured into one of these establishments alone. Not seeing anyone waiting, I didn't see anything wrong with walking up to place my order, almost tasting the cool, vanilla cream before I opened my mouth.

What I did not know was that, at that moment in time, white Southerners' attitudes toward Negroes were hardening. It was September of 1954. School had only been open a few weeks, and the Supreme Court was holding hearings in Washington on its ruling in Brown v. Board of Education of Topeka, Kansas, handed down four months earlier, which had found segregated schools inherently unequal.

The ruling came as an affront to the sanctity of family tradition for white Southerners. They had been raised to believe that the Negro race was impure, that separation of the races worked extremely well and interracial marriage would destroy a civilization. This was an alarm for changes to come.

If a number of black educators in Mississippi feared they would not fare well under integration, and thus were reluctant to embrace the landmark ruling, as some historians have noted, the black teachers of Jefferson Davis County were among the exceptions. Not only did my Aunt Mabel, my primary teacher in elementary school, support Brown v. Board of Education, she had traveled to Kansas to serve as a potential witness in the original case, though she was never called to the witness stand.

Mabel Armstrong was a fiery, heavy-set fat black woman who didn't care what you thought of her. She always spoke up for what she thought was correct. Not the type to harbor selfish interests. Phyllis Norwood, a former high-school sweetheart of mine, worked as a teacher with her and remembers she could curse like a sailor.

The perceived threat to job security held by some black educators in the wake of the Brown decision may not have been far off the mark. In the early 1970s, when integration began to be implemented, Wade Sutton, a Lucas resident and one of four black teachers assigned to the formerly all-white Flora High School in Madison County, was fired for placing a copy of Johnson Publishing Company's *Jet* magazine on a student reading table. Members of his family said it was a *Jet* magazine, although records of the State Sovereignty Commission state that he placed a book of poetry containing "foul and undesirable pornographic material" on the table.

In the early 1940s, there were plenty of small, one-room schools for blacks located in Jefferson Davis County. Most of them were in private cabins or churches. My first school experience was in one of these. However, many one-room schools were consolidated in the early 1950s. Lucas Elementary School, grades one through eight, was one of those multigrade schools with the potbellied stoves used for heat. The teachers would be the first to arrive at school. They would go out back, gather wood from the woodshed, and make fires in the stoves. After that, students maintained the stoves for the day. Partly because of this experience, I would later recognize the meaning of "separate but equal."

The principal at Lucas Elementary was Professor Earnest Lockhart, from the Mt. Olive community. He was also one of my teachers. A wonderful man. He came to the Lucas school after graduation from Jackson State College. He and his beautiful family lived near my family. Even in the early 1950s, he was a freedom fighter. Not only was he president of the Jefferson Davis County Chapter of the National Association for the Advancement of Colored People (NAACP), he also worked closely with Mississippi State Field Secretary Medgar Evers and President C. R. Darden. He participated in national NAACP conventions.

My first intense puppy-love relationship was with the professor's daughter Eunice Lockhart. She was the most beautiful chocolate-looking girl I had ever seen. Her family was friends of ours. We had great times together, sneaking a kiss here and there. There was a trip to the Mississippi State Fair in Jackson that we traveled to on the local school bus. That 125-mile round trip wasn't bad at all. Little did I know that would be the last time I would actually enjoy the back of the bus.

Not long afterward, the disturbing news came that Mississippi segregationists had found out about Eunice's father participating in national and statewide meetings of the NAACP. Records of the Sovereignty Commission indicate that they began to watch him through the work of unnamed informants. They received word that he was passing out literature announcing an NAACP meeting. The state of Mississippi abruptly ended Professor Lockhart's teaching career in the state. He made plans to move his family to Milwaukee, Wisconsin.

Since the family lived only five hundred yards from my house, Eunice walked over to notify me of their leaving on the day before their departure. That was one of the saddest days of my young life. For many years after that, I thought of Eunice. Her mother had been a really good cook at the Lucas school. Willie Armstrong, a cousin of mine, told me once that if he saw Mrs. Lockhart at school on a particular day, he knew he was going to eat well that afternoon. Well, Eunice moved away with her family.

On that unforgettable morning at the Dairy King, I had been on my way to classes at Prentiss Institute, one of only a handful of high schools for blacks in Mississippi. Walking the remaining mile there seemed to take forever.

When you entered that campus, you felt at home. You felt that the place was yours. You owned it. You were a part of making life better for all blacks, and that made you proud.

I had missed my history class. The instructor, Professor J. H.

Armstrong, who was my cousin, was no longer available to discuss the Dairy King issue. That was not a problem, because he would stop by the house that night with a few shirts for Mother to iron. I would speak with him at that time, and when I did, he concluded that I should stay away from that place. No member of my family ever visited the Dairy King again.

High school was easy for me. I enjoyed learning and made good grades. I really didn't need to study very hard, therefore, I failed to develop good study habits. I would pay a price for that later during my first semester in college.

Day-to-day activities at Prentiss Institute were of the black world. The town of Prentiss was of another. What mattered to people in one world generally did not in the other.

The picturesque town, with colorful storefronts and crepe myrtles lining the main thoroughfare, is the county seat. The courthouse (provincial, bright orange brick with white trim) is perched high on the north end of Columbia Avenue. Midway down the drive, the historic Bank of Prentiss stands tall and white with its high porch and Greek Revival pillars. Most of the residents of Prentiss are white. Blacks primarily reside out in the surrounding countryside, although some live in the area back of the business district, known as the Quarters.

On Saturdays, many blacks would come into Prentiss and congregate on a designated street corner on the main strip known as

"Buzzard's Roost," a place comprised of boards nailed together to create wooden benches. It was kept clean Monday through Friday, when blacks were not allowed there. If "too many" blacks sat there during the week, the police would determine that they had better things to do. Saturday was Black Folks Day to sit on those benches. That street corner would be filled with garbage and trash because there was no pick up on Saturdays. It was a street corner where blacks congregated to discuss the next week's farm work. Whites avoided that area on Saturdays like the plague.

The white farmers of Jefferson Davis County were the first in Mississippi to vote against beer after its legalization in 1933. With this same standard of morality five years later, they refused to sanction round dancing in the Community House that had been constructed with federal Works Progress Administration assistance.

The human behavior of avoidance borne of the culture of segregation was of particular interest to Professor Theodore Paige. He was an administrator at my high school, but everybody called him Professor. One Saturday afternoon, I ventured into town and noticed he was parked on the east side of the strip.

All of the parking on Columbia Avenue was on a 45-degree angle, facing the stores. When I approached him to offer a greeting, he invited me to sit in the car with him. After a few moments, he began to explain to me his reason for being there: He was "people watching." His main concern was the interaction of whites and blacks as they approached each other on the sidewalk.

From his people-watching observations, he had concluded that black women (more than black men) took that extra step to avoid getting too close to whites as they passed. On the other hand, black men would speak with white men as they passed more often than black women would. However, his most amazing discovery was that black men did not speak to white women unless they were known to each other.

Professor Paige was serious about this study. He came prepared with his notes, notepads, and other material to document his visits to various small towns where he would observe this behavior.

He concluded that segregation was alive and well in the town of Prentiss. He had observed that whites joyfully displayed their sense of superiority as they sometimes waited for blacks to step off the sidewalks to allow them to pass. Black men realized the high pedestal on which white women were placed, and therefore they did not want to show any familiarity in public. To me, this was odd. I once heard an old white gentleman state: "An open door to (black) education leads to an open (white woman's) bedroom door." Truth be told, that door had been open for a long time.

You didn't second-guess what the instructors said or did at Prentiss Institute, because they knew your mother and father. We were there to get a high-school education and learn a skill or a trade that we could use to become economically self-sufficient.

The founders, Jonas E. Johnson and his wife Bertha LaBranche Johnson, were deputies of Booker T. Washington's philosophy of the power of education, industriousness, and self-reliance. Mrs. Johnson had studied under Washington at Tuskegee Institute. Mr. Johnson, a native of Mississippi, had graduated valedictorian from Alcorn State University, the first land-grant college in the nation, located in the southwestern-most corner of the state. Before settling in Prentiss, Johnson had established a school for blacks in Laurel.

The couple happened to be traveling through Jefferson Davis County when they first arrived with their three small children, and weren't expecting to stay. Seeing it as virgin territory for educating blacks, they put down roots in 1907 and borrowed money to build a school on land once worked by slaves. They received a grant from the all-important Rosenwald fund, established by philanthropist Julius Rosenwald, a Sears and Roebuck Company founder, who helped to build schools for blacks throughout the South. The grant had to be matched by the local community, which in most cases meant that whites also had to buy into the idea of a private school for blacks. Prentiss Institute was licensed as a high school in 1909, and as a junior college in 1932.

So that we could earn a living from the land, we were trained in the science of agriculture. I loved biology. I would choose it later as my major course of study in college, hoping to pursue a career in medicine. I wanted to outsmart the doctor who told me when I was fourteen that I would not live past age twenty-one, because of damage to my heart caused by a bout with rheumatic fever.

"Industrial" in the school's name meant industrial arts, like carpentry, bricklaying, and learning to be a blacksmith or seamstress. "Normal" meant the liberal and fine arts. I learned to play the trombone there. On more than one occasion, I would practice at home by climbing on top of our barn in Lucas and treating the neighbors to free concerts.

Prentiss Institute attracted students from throughout the region and state. By the 1950s, it had grown to include 700 students, forty-plus teachers, and more than twenty buildings, a huge undertaking for the Johnsons in an era when blacks were expected to be subservient to whites.

After establishing the school, both of the Johnsons became influential all over the state. Mr. Johnson organized a statewide "Committee of One Hundred" (COH) in 1923. It was comprised of Mississippi's top 100 advocates for the concerns of Negroes from each of the state's eighty-two counties. Unknown to the masses, the group worked discreetly with white civic leaders to improve black communities. The Johnsons gave the Committee direction, and its strongest participation consistently came from the historically non-plantation areas south of Jackson.

Johnson and his Committee won over Mississippi state legislators by explaining that they were pushing for ways to stop the migration of blacks out of the area. Other white leaders followed.

Had he pressed with his fist, he would have faced a most certain death. Citing the work of the Committee in his definitive *Dark Journey: Black Mississippians in the Age of Jim Crow,* historian Neil McMillen noted, "The organization's patient behind-the-scenes pressure on the white establishment in the 1920s and 1930s helped prepare the way for the more spectacular breakthroughs of a subsequent age."

Long before voter registration drives in the 1960s would enlist some of the poorest of the poor, black Mississippians had known voting. In 1868, there were 86,973 blacks registered; that was 96.7 percent of the total number eligible.

That number began to drop significantly twenty years later with the onset of Jim Crow, and by the 1950s stood at less than 6 percent. Apparently, the obstacles Negroes faced in merely attempting to register to vote had become so overwhelming, most were no longer willing to pay the price.

The Supreme Court's finding of inequality in segregated schools in 1954 energized black voter registration campaigns in the state, which up until then had focused on the small, black middle class in cities. Now, the main leader of the campaigns, the NAACP, moved into rural areas.

At the same time, the White Citizen's Council, vowing to prevent any semblance of integration, was appealing to the white middle class in towns and villages in the wake of the Brown v. Board of Education Supreme Court decision. Following in footsteps made by their parents' generation, which had instituted Jim Crow laws, the legislature added more restrictions to voter registration in 1954, requiring applicants to write a "reasonable" interpretation of a section of the state constitution.

As a young boy, I learned through family discussions that if more blacks demanded their right to vote, things could change in Mississippi. Medgar Evers and Aaron Henry, the state's NAACP leaders, knew this, and acted upon that premise. It was their example that would later move me to begin to question my freedom, to ponder the measure of man I would seek to become.

In 1955, the number of black Mississippians registered to vote was 21,502, about 4 percent of the voting age population. White registered voters totaled 423,456, or 59.6 percent of those eligible.

If the percentage of black voters wasn't paltry enough, the next year, huge numbers of them were suddenly and arbitrarily stricken from the rolls in several counties. That was two years after the Brown v. Board Supreme Court ruling in 1956, the same year in which the Mississippi legislature established the State Sovereignty Commission. Historian John Dittmer has described the agency as a secret police force that operated like a small-time FBI, placing informants and spies in civil-rights groups to thwart their efforts, and owing its allegiance to the White Citizens' Council. The Commission was very much at work in the late 1950s, although most people did not know it existed.

The total number of blacks registered in Jefferson Davis County was 1,221 before the rolls were purged in 1956; afterward, that number decreased to 50.

To the more than 1,000 Negroes who were disenfranchised, county Circuit Clerk James W. Daniels offered a useless explanation: "No one here has been refused the right to vote because of race or color. They have been refused because they have failed to qualify under the laws of Mississippi."

I am forever bound to Jefferson Davis County, if not for being born there, then for the actions of Circuit Clerk Daniel. It was essentially his actions that year that would later order my steps into the movement.

Mississippi State Sovereignty Commission records made public in 1998, more than forty years later, revealed that its investigators were in communication with Jefferson Davis County officials in 1956, and suspected names of NAACP members were removed from the voter rolls by Circuit Clerk Daniel.

According to the declassified records, Daniel had received a stolen NAACP "Minute Book" from unnamed informants, and he spied upon the general community. Of course, the Commission was passing that information along to the White Citizens' Council.

Daniel and the sheriff of Jefferson Davis County, Shelby Mikell, as well as other unnamed informants, gave the Sovereignty Commission various reports about the "racial situation" in the county. In one documented exchange, Daniel and Mikell told an investigator that the NAACP was operating underground in Prentiss. In another, they stated that they suspected Prentiss Institute of being a "hotbed" of NAACP activity. The Johnson's son, A. L., who was being groomed to take over the school's operation, was suspected of being involved, thereby minimizing his parents' accomodationist approach to race relations.

In addition to local officials and the unnamed informants, the Federal Bureau of Investigation was supplying information to the Sovereignty Commission about race relations in Jefferson Davis County.

One year later, Aaron Henry, the state president of the NAACP, launched a statewide registration drive to counter the precipitous drop in registered black voters. Classes were conducted to teach blacks more about the state constitution in an attempt to get larger numbers to register. Henry wanted to register 100,000 black voters in the state, the catastrophic number estimated to have been purged the previous year.

State law provided that any citizen could register at any time during the year, and the NAACP encouraged Negroes to register with regularity. However, due to the stringent qualification law, it was still difficult for blacks to register in certain areas.

Rev. H. D. Darby was one of the Negro voters who had been dropped from the rolls in Jefferson Davis County. He had moved his family to Prentiss from Laurel some ten years earlier to give his children a high-school education. The family lived in a farmhouse on the campus of Prentiss Institute. Five of the children became students there.

Darby made at least four attempts to re-register to vote in 1957, but each time the circuit clerk would not permit him. Others who had been previously disqualified also returned, and were met with the same results. That year, Darby became actively involved in the Jefferson Davis County NAACP.

He had lived through having his reputation smeared by local whites. A minister by profession, he also sold cosmetics, and was accused of being a ladies' man.

Fed up with all the mockery and intimidation, Darby filed a federal lawsuit in March of 1958, challenging, for the first time in the history of the state of Mississippi, the rigid restrictions on blacks who attempted to register to vote. With the assistance of the NAACP legal department, Darby sought to have such rules declared unconstitutional. It was the first lawsuit of its kind to be filed under federal provisions of the civil rights law passed by Congress in 1957.

The NAACP had offered to help Negroes anywhere in Mississippi sue for violation of their voting rights. After Darby responded to the call in Jefferson Davis County, he was celebrated as Man of the Year at a state meeting of the NAACP in Clarksdale.

The public hearing of Darby's voting case was carried out in the courtroom of the federal building in Jackson. Negroes from throughout Mississippi sat there in rapt attention. Constance Baker Motley, of New York City, and R. Jess Brown, of Jackson, were attorneys for the plaintiff. The decision of the three-judge panel, presided over by federal judge Ben Cameron of the United States Court of Appeals for the Fifth Circuit, rendered a negative decision that left Mississippi's stringent law intact. The NAACP Legal Defense and Educational Fund declined to appeal to the Supreme Court and indicated that the case would be turned over to the Civil Rights Commission instead.

Having witnessed basic rights of citizenship being taken away from members of my family, teachers, and others I knew, coupled with the anger of being cut down to size just when I was beginning to notice myself within the world around me, reinforced in my young mind the cruelty of segregation, bias, and hate.

That this was considered normal, increasingly struck me as inhumane. White citizens marched proudly to their "whites only" water fountains, restaurants, schools, and churches. Blacks moved to a different beat, were usually in poor health, undereducated, and were eligible for few, if any, choices to support themselves other than working for meager earnings. This "normalcy" was never full of anything but inequity.

The situation was affecting how people lived in and around Lucas. Most of our residents were very poor. Some could not secure loans to continue their farming operations. It wasn't too difficult for them to make the decision to leave the state in search of higher-paying jobs in the industrial north. The knowledge of all these things instilled in me the burning fire of "change." We could not wait for a new organization or new directions. We were mandated by fate to use the tools that we had and make them more aggressive. We needed to fortify our dedication and loyalty to the cause. We needed a new way of fighting racism.

All of this remained heavy on my mind.

2

The Environment

BLACK MISSISSIPPIANS RESISTED THE undoing of their rights as American citizens through every practical means available to them. The early freedmen who set out to establish all-black towns, like Lucas, were publicly affirming their personal dignity and self-worth.

These were places where blacks could gain back their respect. They did not have to wait for a cashier to finish serving white folks before they were served. They did not have to get off the sidewalk to let someone else pass.

In Lucas, we were proud to express our knowledge of our history. We were taught that our ancestors believed they could govern themselves as effectively as, if not better than, the white establishment. We thought of our founders as forthright people, determined to advance themselves and their future.

Unfortunately, the price of that all-important commodity, cotton, began to bottom out in the early twentieth century, and by the mid-1950s, many all-black towns were suffering severe economic decline. Mound Bayou, one of the largest such towns in the Delta region to the north of us, managed to survive. For a while, Lucas did as well.

The westward journey across South Mississippi, along U.S. 84, carried travelers into the heart of our small village, which could be found rising from flatlands about five miles outside of Prentiss. Cars approached heading into a curve marked by a no-passing sign and another that read simply, "Lucas." People were often walking or crossing that stretch of the road. Most cars would slow down. Nevertheless, accidents did occur. One Sunday, when I was five, I witnessed the tragic loss of a cousin, Shirley Maud Collins, who was one year older than I. She was struck and killed as she ran home from church.

The fifty or more households in Lucas were bound by a handful of locally owned shops and stores. Most families owned a truck; very few did not have a vehicle in which to get around. The highway divided the community into halves; even so, we were like one big family. Furthermore, we were each descended from a small group of freedmen, which meant that most of us were related to each other.

The resilience of the black Southerner in the face of a separate and unequal society lay in the talent and resourcefulness acquired in managing to survive.

Our teachers, cultivated and confident, were not unlike leaders in the community. They made it their business to teach the younger ones what they knew. The same was true for almost any adult in our world: the church fathers, Sunday School teachers, our parents, the athletic coaches, and older guys in the neighborhood who challenged and guided us into maturity.

Teachers confirmed their belief in us, they pushed us to excel. My primary teacher in elementary school was Aunt Mabel, who kept a close eye on me. If I misbehaved, she would take care of me, and she never failed to tell my mother, Aunt Vaudra. After all of that, my favorite uncle, Alonzo Armstrong, would find out and chastise me all day long. As I can remember, I misbehaved only once or twice. Needless to say, I was a model student. I was smart and I excelled academically. Because of Aunt Mabel's skill, I was allowed to bypass one grade level.

Our teachers' high expectations, together with the nurturing and learning we received at home, created an environment that bred not only survival, but growth and achievement. The cumulative effect spawned a vitality that averted the white supremacist's intention of rendering us inferior.

Professor J. H. Armstrong, my mother's cousin, and his wife Adella Topps-Armstrong, ran a country store with a hand-pump gas tank outside. They sold a few groceries and other supply items. The majority of their customers made most of their purchases on credit. The couple was generous in extending credit, their son would inform me years later.

The professor and his wife alternated their schedules so one could operate the store while the other was teaching school or was busy elsewhere. He was a graduate of both Rust College and Tuskegee Institute. He taught history at Prentiss Institute, where at one point he was appointed principal. Cousin Adella was both an elementary-school teacher and midwife.

Professor Armstrong wore one more hat: he was an ordained minister. He was exceptionally knowledgeable and straightforward, and rarely did I ever hear him raise his voice. Like his occasional sermons, his high-school lectures were spoken in a quiet monotone, which I admired, because I, too, was a quiet person, and I had been blessed with a conversational ability to influence other people.

The professor's example would inspire me later in life to teach my two daughters and granddaughter that one need not shout to be heard. "Speak softly, but with meaning," I'd tell them. "When you make a promise, do so quietly. And always keep it."

Such were the lessons I learned from the elders in Lucas, who also shared their skills and talents with the younger ones. As the fortunate recipients of their knowledge, we would make time to watch and listen. For example, it was nothing to find a bunch of kids hanging out with the local blacksmith, Hew Norwood, on a Saturday evening. We were amazed at what he could do. Plus, he had a gorgeous granddaughter.

He would have on his dark, fire-resistant apron, and talk to me while sharpening the blade of a hoe or other farm tool brought into the shop. Many a customer would come in with a misshapen tool, not knowing specifically what they wanted done. He'd make it for them, whatever they needed: handles for hammers and axes, or rounder, sturdier wagon wheels.

At the start of fall, the men in Lucas would set the date to round up the boys and supply the elderly, disabled, and the elementary school with enough firewood to last through winter. They'd call for us to meet early on a Saturday morning. After the wood was gathered and cut, the boys carried and stacked most of it wherever it was supposed to go. Sometimes it seemed we stacked enough wood to last a couple of years. It was the elders' way of teaching us to be responsible community members.

We didn't talk about white folks much, mainly because there weren't any around. The closest ones lived two miles west along the highway in a town called Silver Creek. It was relatively close, but just inside the boundary of the next county, Lawrence, whose population was mostly white and whose history dated well back into the period of slavery.

Silver Creek had more businesses and larger stores than Lucas. The number of residents was twice that of our community, albeit still small, around 200. It was commonly mentioned by blacks in our area that the Ku Klux Klan was well represented there.

There was one bank in Silver Creek. In addition to the local residents, it served the people of Lucas and other nearby black communities, such as Spring Hill and New Hebron. At least once a year, my father or his brother would finance a new truck at that bank for use in their logging business. They would just walk in and say they needed to borrow the cost of the vehicle. The loan would be processed to be paid monthly or quarterly.

Dad would purchase his vehicles at the one General Motors dealer in Silver Creek. He would purchase a GMC truck, and his brother Clark would purchase a Chevrolet. The brothers had a "running argument" about whose truck was better. George Armstrong, a cousin, always purchased Dodge trucks for his operation. On the weekends when those three got together, the arguments were so loud, you would think they were angry at each other. None of the three ever won. Their truck stories were a match for "fish tales."

Though I did not know it at that time, there was a Caucasian businessman in Silver Creek who became a trusted friend of my father. His name will not be mentioned here to protect the interests of family members. Some Saturday nights, many of the white men from the area would sit around his shop to talk and drink. Some were known Klan members. If decisions had been made in those meetings that were related to people in Lucas, Dad's friend would pay us a visit. He interacted with us free of any bias. Compared to most whites with whom we came in contact, he was an exception. I know now that there were others like him.

On the other hand, the tragedy of racial terrorism was not lost on members of my family. The image of my disabled uncle, Ransom A. Armstrong, was seared into my young mind. Older relatives told me the story: one day, a bunch of white men waited on a wooden bridge along the highway that ran through Lucas. When my Uncle Ransom came riding along on his horse, they intimidated that horse so much, it became frightened and threw my uncle over the side of the bridge. He suffered permanent brain damage in the fall; he was never the same after that.

Another family story involved my grandfather, Thomas Edison Armstrong, Sr. Angry white mobs in the area attempted to lynch him, not once, but twice. Most people thought he married a white woman, Annie Evans Sutton, but my paternal grandmother was, in fact, a mulatto. She rescued her husband in both incidents. In one case, she is said to have convinced the crowd that she was not a

Caucasian who had married a Negro, but that she was also a Negro. Although I did not witness these acts of racial brutality, the question of why they happened always lingered.

Most weekends, Dad drove his truck into Silver Creek, and I went with him, usually to pick up a few items in the stores or pay a bill. Occasionally, Mother would go with us. During the short drive, I would ask her if the bad people who tried to hurt my uncle and grandfather were still there. She would say, "Don't ever talk about that." I was never allowed to speak of those family tragedies until I reached manhood.

I think most of the young men my age cried when we learned, in the end days of the summer of 1955, about the shocking murder of Emmett Till. I was born in 1941, as was he. But Emmett was from Chicago and apparently didn't realize different codes of conduct applied in Mississippi, where he was visiting relatives. He supposedly flirted with or whistled at Carolyn Bryant, a twenty-one-year-old white woman who was married to an owner of a small store. Her husband, Roy, and his half-brother grabbed fourteen-year-old Emmett from his great-uncle's house. They took him to a barn, beat him, gouged out one of his eyes, and according to his mother, Mamie Till, someone used an axe to split open his head, and then they shot him through the head. They got rid of his body by tying a seventy-pound cotton gin fan around his neck with barbed wire and throwing his mutilated remains into the Tallahatchie River. Young black men in Mississippi at that time understood that any one of us could have been in that situation, just because of a wolf whistle at a white girl.

Black Mississippians did not accept such violent hatred lying down. What did they do? Never losing their self-respect, they put on their game face. They survived by becoming some of the greatest actors in the world.

Whenever they ventured beyond the confines of their communities, they worked hard to maintain that exhaustive game face. They were instilled with the wisdom of their ancestors, who tempered the rage of oppression with the expectation that, if they didn't object, their children would live to see a better life. Though the older generation knew they had a specific purpose for the performance, the pain of pretending never lessened.

More and more, I have come to understand why my mother thought her father finally gave up on life. The constant pretending wore down his spirit. He began to lose his self-respect. He was no longer capable of looking his ten children in the eye as he bore the burden of humiliation, and would say, "I was doing that for you."

My parents were great role players when they needed to be. They knew that it was easier to let white folks think they were satisfied with conditions as they were. They knew that if they alone rejected those conditions, they could no longer feed their families. They would no longer be able to get loans for new trucks, the best prices for logs or pulpwood, nor to have the peace of mind in knowing they could transport a load of logs without getting a traffic ticket. They knew they were the source of income for other blacks in the community who had to feed their families, so they played the role.

The Klan was known to exist in our area, so black homeowners almost always kept a firearm within reach; if the Klan ever attacked a family or one of its members, the cowards who covered their faces would not live to talk about it.

One night, one of the horses that Dad used in his logging business escaped from the barn and ran out on the highway into the path of a truck, and was hit and killed. The white male driver of the truck became incensed, and warned that he and his friends would return. Dad and I camped outside the house for two nights with rifles and shotguns.

He put me on notice to be ready with my crack shot: "They will probably have sheets on, and we don't want to hurt anyone, but if they come into the yard, see that they don't leave." I shrugged, somewhat disagreeing with him, yet felt it was better to be alive than dead. Had the men returned, no matter what the outcome may have been, I know that I would not be here today. We had only a few guns and could have been easily outnumbered.

Thousands of black Mississippians were migrating north in the early 1950s. At the same time, thousands, if not more, never gave a thought to leaving. Those in the latter group were usually landowners, the people who loved the land.

Put simply: land had been too hard to come by to walk away and leave it. We had been descended from an enslaved people for whom possession of the ground they farmed was equivalent to freedom.

I think my dad would have died a quick death if someone had taken his land. Next to his mother and wife, his forty acres was his life. Our family had inherited an additional forty acres from my birth-father's ancestors, which was adjacent to the land Dad owned.

As much as Dad loved the land, he hated farming. Be that as it may, he would still plant three acres of cotton every year. He didn't care if he made three bales or zero bales. To make use of the land was a measure of responsibility, and it demonstrated economic independence. The fact that he could go outside and spit on what belonged to him mattered. He wasn't the only one.

My mother's first cousin Willie Armstrong, who lived next to us, loved his property so much he would go outside and preach to the land, the cows, and the horses: they had been so good to him. In all other ways he was fine, but occasionally, he loved to preach to his belongings.

The little farming Dad did was just enough to cover living expenses: food for the table, hay for the horses and cattle. The cattle herd amounted to 30–50 head at any one time, and included Brahman, the ones with humps on their backs. The only reason Dad bred that type was because he loved to look at them. The Brahman bull we owned was the meanest I'd ever seen. If he saw you walking in the pasture, he'd take off and chase you.

I learned to drive at age eight, standing on my feet in the cab of a tandem-axle truck. My legs were too short to reach the accelerator and brakes sitting down, so Dad would instruct me, as I stood against the seat, to steer the truck around the fields and pastures on our farm.

By age twelve, I had been driving for some time, and would sometimes transport the horses to Dad's work site the night before he needed them. Driving a one-ton Ford pickup, I would make two trips with two horses each time, and then rope off the staging area. When all the timber was cut, I would go back and get them.

Dad always kept two large mules and four huge Clydesdale horses, all of which he needed to operate his logging business. Sometimes, the two mules would be used for tilling the soil in the garden and hay fields; Dad would hire someone to do that sort of work. On Saturdays, I would help, using one of the horses or one of the two mules to plow. Some of my cousins would come over to help.

One of the funniest things I ever saw was when Mother took it upon herself to try to teach me how to hold a plow. She had watched Dad do it, but she'd never tilled the soil a day in her life. That plow was snapping her from side to side like a wet towel. I couldn't stop laughing for two straight hours.

The three acres of cotton we had were to give my sister, Nellie, and me "something to do." Agility and quickness of speed were required to produce a sack of cotton that amounted to something. I never scored well in that department. Even the incentive of earning some money didn't make a difference. One time, I joined cousins Eddie, James, and Willie C.—Uncle Nemirah's sons—to pick some cotton on another man's farm. They picked enough to make the trip worthwhile, but I could have stayed at home, as I finished the day with a total of just ninety pounds. Another cousin of mine, Shelton Lucas, could pick 300 pounds in a day.

My mother could not pick cotton either. Dad claimed we had "too much white folks in us," his way of saying we couldn't do it correctly. By the same token, he couldn't pick cotton any better than Mother and I could. After I watched him tire of trying a few times, I knew exactly why he chose to be a logger. But we did manage to grow plenty of food. Some of our relatives grew fruit. Mother—like all the women of the community—spent long hours canning food for the winter.

On Sunday mornings, my parents, Nellie, and I would prepare to leave the house together and walk to church. Lucas Tabernacle Church of Christ Holiness remains one of the few remaining vestiges of history in Lucas. In my grandparents' time, the congregation had split from Shady Grove Baptist Church, the oldest church in the community, following a fiery preacher who stood in a wagon that served as his pulpit.

Our house faced the highway. As we walked out toward the church, Dad would turn and go in the opposite direction toward Silver Creek. Sometimes, Dad would go to church with us instead, such as the time he was excommunicated from Lucas Tabernacle for smoking. He enjoyed his Camel cigarettes.

After the service, you could catch up on the latest news in the community and talk to people you hadn't seen or heard from in a while. The after-church activity was like a town hall meeting.

I first learned of Tougaloo College at church. Dr. William Bender, who did outreach for the college, spoke to my parents about visiting the campus, telling them to be sure to ask for Mr. H. E. Dockins, who was the registrar. Mom and Dad wanted nothing more than for my sister and me to attend Tougaloo.

Jonas Johnson, the face of Prentiss Institute in the community, also made regular appearances at various local black churches, where he would spread the news about what was happening at the beloved high school for blacks. Parents could make arrangements with him to get their children admitted to the school.

Dad pretty much left it up to Mom to raise me; still, he was there to back her up. Mom's word was gospel. Though she was seven years older than Dad, Mom was somewhat more modern in her thinking.

Everybody was wild about B.B. King, who was just breaking out in the midfifties. When he was scheduled to perform for the first time at the black Masonic Hall in Jackson, my sister, who was in high school, begged Dad to let her go with her friends. Of course, he was of a different mind. It was only after Mom stepped in that Nellie got her wish to go.

There is no questioning the fact that Mom raised me to be a gentleman in true Southern fashion. She insisted that I address a lady respectfully, with the title "Miss" or "Mrs." She encouraged me to offer my help to ladies I passed by in the community.

I soon learned that women talked to each other. Therefore, if I did a favor for one, whether she was young or an older lady, the whole community would eventually hear of it and offer praises. Almost every time I saw a woman I had but one thing to say: "What can I do for you?" I swear, Bob Dylan could have gotten the title of his song from me. Maybe I told him that story when we met in 1961.

Before long, all the women in the community were telling each other that I was "such a nice boy." Of course, all this worked to my benefit.

I'll never forget Mother's advice to me once I began to think of having a girlfriend: "Never become sexually active with a girl if you don't wish to marry her." I adhered to that policy.

Most of the best-looking girls in the community were relatives. A few were not, and I found them. We called almost everyone "cousin" so we didn't address a potentially unknown relative incorrectly. Consequently, the exchange signaled the taboo associated with developing romantic feelings with a person of kin.

One of the first girls I dreamed of kissing was a young lady named Princess Uston. Lo and behold, her mother and my father were cousins. Kinship ruined my chances with her.

On the occasions when I took a female friend out on a date, we traveled in Dad's tandem-axle log truck. It made for interesting conversations.

Eleanor Bridges never had a problem with my mode of transportation. She had a great personality. She lived nine miles away in Lawrence County and attended a different high school. I would only see her on some weekends. Those days were wonderful. Sometimes, I would visit her church, Pearl River Valley Baptist, then take her home in the log truck. I brought her home a few times. We'd sit in the swing on the porch. Mother liked Ella, and she thought we would get married.

We didn't, and along came Phyllis McInnis, my pride and joy. We saw each other almost every day at Prentiss Institute, where she came in as a freshman during my second year. One memorable moment was the high-school prom. By this time, Mother had become impatient with the noise and other peculiarities of riding in the log truck, and talked Dad into purchasing a 1956 Ford automobile. That was the car I happily drove to pick up Phyllis, my prom date. We were stunned to learn that two hours prior to our arrival, one of our schoolmates had been killed after driving off a bridge near the school. Another student who was a passenger was seriously injured. No high-school prom was sadder than ours.

We were sweethearts for most of our three years together in high school. Then out of the blue, on the last day of school, I saw her with another guy. It was over, as far as I was concerned. The betrayal cut me to the quick, but it wasn't the sort of thing I would take to my Dad—even if he was one of the kindest, most generous humanitarians I have ever known.

Our family did not "need" a whole lot. We were an island in a sea of poverty. My father made a little money in his logging business, but he wasn't in it for himself. After caring for his family, Enoch Barnes' top priority was to help the common man. People often came to him looking for jobs, or for help with financial emergencies. He wasn't what you'd call wealthy, but he'd give you one-half of his last dollar. Nellie and I saw him do it many times. When we questioned him, he would only say, "I know that I can get some more." He would often tell my sister and me "You may be broke, but always know where you can get some money if you really need it." We both put that into practice, with good credit ratings as well as good business and personal relationships.

He wanted things to change in Mississippi. It saddened him to realize that he didn't have the education he needed to make the changes he wanted to see. He promised himself that he would support whoever was on the front lines of the struggle for the legal protection of civil rights. He had no idea, of course, that I would get on that battlefield. When he learned of it, he would caution me fervently, "Son, get a hold of yourself," and ask, "Are you making some kind of death wish?"

One of Dad's favorite sayings was, "Do the best you can." He was born in 1909, and as I mentioned, he was taken out of school at a young age. I have no idea how he learned to do math since he did not receive a proper education, but he could add and subtract better and faster in his head than Nellie and I could with pencil and paper. However, he could not read well.

He always knew when he was being cheated, or not given the best price for his logs. Once, instead of taking his loads of logs to the sawmills of Monticello or Brookhaven, he began taking them to the small towns of Georgetown, Hazlehurst, and Wanilla, where he received more money. When he was asked about this by the white folks, he simply stated, "They pay me more money." Soon after that, the owners of the sawmills at Monticello and Brookhaven began paying him more.

It was not difficult for Dad to find workers to hire in his business. Black unemployment was extremely high. The regular workers would show up at our house every morning of the week, no matter what, and bang on the door by 5:30 AM, alerting everybody in the house. Typically, a few newer workers would not get there as early as scheduled and some negotiation would ensue over how soon they could start.

One cousin would work with my father every day. He would be paid on Friday afternoon, and by 11:00 PM on Saturday night, he'd be back at the door to borrow ten dollars. He'd have spent his money on whiskey (most of the state was dry, but a bottle of "bootleg" could be easily found). My sister would get upset with Dad for always lending him money.

The logging routine was consistent. The jobsite would change, but the task was the same with each rotation. Dad and his brother Clark would cut the timber and haul it off to the sawmill. Each employed one full-time driver and one part-time driver. Their brother, Uncle Nemirah, was one of the regular truck drivers. The two brothers hired other men to drive the trucks, operate the mule teams, and cut the timber with crosscut saws, two men to a saw, alternating the pull. They paid the guys well. The regular workers earned enough money to support their families.

Enoch and Clark could look at a "stand" of timber and tell you how many loads of logs and pulpwood it would yield. I was never very good at that.

Because many white Mississippians were selling their timber and land and moving north in the early 1950s, Dad and Uncle Clark were required to purchase large tracts to get the timber. Ordinarily, the rules of the trade allowed access by just purchasing the timber.

The brothers made many land purchases. One year, they bought a 360-acre tract of land. After cutting the timber, they decided to plant watermelons in one of the huge fields. Tilling that land took courage. It was richly fertile, in a low-lying area near a swamp, the kind of land where one could expect to plow up nests of snakes. When that happened, someone would inevitably run across the field, screaming, "Snakes! Snakes!"

All the brothers' children, nieces, and nephews helped tend those watermelons. When they grew ripe and were taken to the market to be sold, the profit was barely enough to cover expenses. The brothers didn't plant any more, and sold the land the next summer.

Dinnertime at our house was the most likely time our relatives would stop by to visit. Mother kept something going with Uncle Clark's wife, Marthan; they were cousins and had married brothers. Aunt Mabel was also a familiar presence, and frequently made a fuss about the consistently poor quality of any supplies she was able to get from the school board in Jefferson Davis County. She was never one to forget a birthday, though. She knew everybody's, and everybody's children's birthdays.

Mother loved to cook, and dinner usually consisted of a full-course meal. There would often be black-eyed peas and cornbread, squash or potatoes, chicken and rice. As we ate together, Dad would share some of his concerns: a cousin who was unable to get a loan; someone else needed bond money to get their son out of jail; another lady asked if her son could come live with us. He would offer room and board from time to time to such persons, as well as the occasional worker who traveled from afar.

After his wife passed away, Professor Armstrong visited almost daily. He was a cousin of Mother's. He would bring his white shirts to our house and ask to iron them. He would bring one shirt at a time, and never compensated my mother one penny. My sister would get so angry with him, especially if Mother was busy and instructed *her* to iron the shirt. My father, who hated snobbery, thought of Professor Armstrong as the most down-to-earth educated person he knew.

There were days when Dad would go to work in the morning, come home in the evening, eat, dress, and disappear. Mother would say that he had gone to lend his support to the causes of the "learned black folks."

I found out what she was speaking of when I gained access to the files of the Mississippi State Sovereignty Commission some fifty years later. The revelation lay in the NAACP Minute Book that had been confiscated by the circuit clerk of Jefferson Davis County and given to Commission investigators. No one knew it at the time, but the Commission had been keeping track of individuals who attended NAACP meetings. When I saw that complete document of some 200 names, I couldn't take my eyes away; I studied it with great interest, anxious to learn the identities of these freedom soldiers who'd been unknown to me at the time.

They were the very heroes who helped shape my life. The list included J. H. "Joseph" Armstrong, Alonzo Ball, Enoch and Clark Barnes, Ernest Lockhart, Victoria Sutton, E. L. Washington, Willie Mae Warner, and Mabel Armstrong.

All the people listed in that book were people moving to the beat of drums for freedom. No one ever told me about their quiet resistance, because I was considered too young to be trusted with such weighty information. The mere mention of NAACP could invite trouble into one's home. Therefore, it was just not spoken of openly, especially in the rural areas.

Interestingly, I also learned later that the Sovereignty Commission kept a record on Professor Armstrong during the time he was principal of Prentiss Institute. Apparently, he became a target due to his six-month subscription to the *Jackson Advocate*, a black newspaper, along with his candidacy for the lily-white Jefferson Davis County Board of Education.

3

~

Education of
the Mississippi Negro

I WAS A STUDENT AT TOUGALOO COLLEGE in 1958 when I first became aware of the struggle to protect civil rights, and I was moved to join the NAACP and volunteer to become a field worker. The primary objective of the movement in Mississippi was to mobilize more blacks to register to vote.

At that time, it was commonly known that less than 5 percent of black Mississippians were registered. To create public outrage over the indignation blacks faced when they attempted to register, the NAACP began sending organizers—sometimes alone, but mostly in groups of two—into the small towns and hamlets throughout the state, to begin the very dangerous and difficult task of organizing and training black residents to stand up to the insults they knew they would encounter.

Simply registering to vote did not just require confronting the intimidating tactics of a county registrar or other whites in the vicinity: you also had to give a written or oral interpretation of a section of the state constitution. Different registrars could choose different sections. Besides that, any black who asserted his or her rights in this way was likely to be fired, evicted, denied credit, beaten, experience a fire-bombing of the family home, or be killed.

A tiny black middle class, comprised of school teachers, independent business people, and those who had been able to retain ownership of land, was fully intimidated as well. Among them were a few courageous individuals who stood up for their rights and those of others.

There was always the question: What could be done to get more blacks to break through such a rigid barrier? Then, if that were accomplished, what good would it do?

Only in the South did black Americans face a dichotomy of home and heart. Medgar Evers was fond of saying, "We love the land, same as any Southerner, but, we love first-class citizenship best."

The Tougaloo experience taught me that freedom was only a short distance away. It was up to me to go and find it.

The college has a long tradition of upholding the principles of dignity of the human being and the right to equal treatment under the law. It was founded by the American Missionary Association in 1869, not long after a time when teaching enslaved blacks had been extremely dangerous.

Historic Tougaloo, located northwest of the state capitol of Jackson, rests on a 500-acre campus anchored by giant, old oak trees, draped in falls of Spanish moss. A private college, it is regarded as something of an oasis amidst the harsh realities of the racial divide that has existed in Mississippi. Students are provided a classical, liberal arts education. The faculty is progressive in its teaching. The professors, many of them white and imported from East Coast schools, usually have religious and/or political beliefs that support racial equality.

Among the faculty members during my time there, Dr. Ernst Borinski, a sociologist and one of the top writers and thinkers in his field, allowed students free rein to express ideas about black civil rights. He was one of about fifty Jewish scholars who fled Nazi Germany and taught in historically black colleges in the United States. Looking back on his influence at Tougaloo, Dr. Joyce Ladner, a dear classmate with whom I worked in the movement, recalled, "Borinski had an affinity with blacks, because Jews experienced a similar persecution." She is, herself, a widely recognized scholar who became the first female president of Howard University in Washington, D.C.

Borinski, who stayed at Tougaloo for thirty-five years, helped to establish the college's reputation for rejecting the system of racial exclusion. Working with then-chaplain Rev. John Mangrum, Borinski set up an exchange program with students at Millsaps, the white Methodist college in Jackson.

In addition to the exchange with Millsaps, the administration at Tougaloo admitted a few Northern white students to its campus. Reacting to a report in Jackson's daily newspaper about the latter move, local whites dubbed the college "Cancer College," for its "integration" and progressive ideas.

A small group of students at Tougaloo, only about fifteen or twenty of approximately 350 students, initiated the first public civil-rights demonstrations in Mississippi. Working with the NAACP in 1961, we launched sit-ins, picketing, and boycotting of stores that refused to serve or hire blacks. Our student activism kept pace with the national movement, culminating in the work of the Student Nonviolent Coordinating Committee (SNCC), and effectively established a tradition of activism at Tougaloo. Because the college is private, we were able to act with less fear of reprisal than our counterparts at state-supported black universities.

I always knew there could never be justification for the evil forced upon us in the South. I also knew that we would succeed in our efforts to clear the way for blacks in Mississippi to be treated as citizens in a democratic society, free of fear and intimidation. However,

I felt that we needed a new vehicle for change.

My break from the reasoning of the past began in the fall of 1958, sitting in a mass meeting held in a black church in Jackson. One typically went to these meetings to follow the freedom movement. I was a mere freshman when a friend and I decided to go to one at Pearl Street African Methodist Episcopal Church on September 23, 1958. Naturally, having moved to the city from a rural community, where there was no open discussion of the movement, I was curious.

They started off singing electrifying freedom songs! People were clapping and rocking! When you walked out of there, you'd be ready to get involved—Ain't Gonna Let Nobody Turn Me Around!

Little did I know then that while I was enjoying the meeting, blissfully unaware, representatives of the Sovereignty Commission were outside recording the license numbers of all the cars in the parking lot.

Because there weren't a lot of people from Tougaloo or anywhere in the state or country participating in the movement, I took notes on what was said at all the meetings I attended. I knew that something extraordinary was happening, and I went to each and every meeting I possibly could. What follows summarizes the content of a printed program from one meeting and my personal notes.

Mass Meeting

The program included a twelve-year-old girl who had been arrested for boarding the front seat of a bus, and was presented as follows:

Program

Guest: **LILLIAN SMITH—Author, "Whiteman and his Conscience"**

Devotion by: **REVEREND PAUL BROOKS**

Prayer Song: **WE SHALL OVERCOME**

Introduction of young Ms. Jessie Divins: **STORY OF HER ARREST**

Ms. Jessie Divins, age 12, a student at Campbell High School, was arrested for boarding a bus in Mississippi for an unknown destination. She was asked by the bus driver and eventually the police to move to the back. She did not. She was placed under arrest, removed from the bus, and taken to jail. At trial, Ms. Divins explained to the judge that she had boarded the bus and sat in the front seat. The judge told her that if she came before him again, he would send her to "Oakland" [Oakley Training School]. She informed the judge that she did not mind going to Oakland, and every trip that she would make would be made sitting on the front seat of a bus.

Announcement

Ruben Martin, twenty-two-year-old polio victim, was arrested and charged with drunkenness. Needs help.

Speaker: MINISTER R. L. T. SMITH

Three-part Subject:

1] One God and his Holy Word—"Our Bible".

2] The Constitution of the United States of America

3] I Love Mississippi, but I love first class citizenship best.

We as a people have been denied the rights of the constitution too many times. Segregation teaches "hate and inferiority." The Mississippi Citizens Council is a "dog council" organized by two ministers. We owe it to God, state, and country to help to "find" ourselves. Whites in this country feel superior to all other races. We must love them if we expect them to love us. This task requires faith, courage, and love. Segregation must go. Citizens must be protected. We must use our selective buying and selling power. God can help us destroy hate, bigotry, and segregation. Become aware of your rights as citizens of the United States. We want to

walk in dignity. Walk like a man. Talk like a man. Get all
the education that's possible. Our forefathers worked
very hard for this country. Their money was taken to help
build medical and law schools. Please join hands, hearts,
and intelligence. Their ministers are speaking from a theological throne. They never come down and say, "You must
love everybody."

We must examine ourselves first. We must act "first
class." Stop jumping and hollering. Leave all the old bun
dles at home. Sit down and shut your mouths. Leave your
lunch buckets at home. Who wants to sit beside someone
who is salivating and chewing tobacco? If we keep Christ
in our hearts, we can't fail. Be mindful that God is
no respecter of persons. He loves Governor Ross
Barnett just as well as you. We need men to tell the
world what we want. How can three people tell what all
Negroes want? Everybody needs to speak up. So many
people haven't done anything to support the cause.
It's always that faithful few. If they can create
laws to help bring factories to Mississippi, then they
can help bring peace to Mississippi. Pick up posters
today at 6 PM for 8:00 AM tomorrow, Saturday.

At another mass meeting later that fall, I stayed afterward to meet Medgar Evers, the NAACP field secretary for the state of Mississippi.

During the program, he had read some familiar names of people I knew back home in Jefferson Davis County—some of my relatives and family friends—and other places, saying they were among hundreds of eligible black voters who had been arbitrarily stricken from county voting rolls.

Until that moment, I had been unaware of the 1956 catastrophe that had occurred in my home county. I also learned of the unprecedented federal lawsuit challenging the constitutionality of Mississippi's voting eligibility laws. It had been filed in 1958 while I was still in high school, by a man who resided on the campus of black Prentiss Institute, Rev. H. D. Darby.

Hearing all of this for the first time, after another powerful boost of singing freedom songs, prompted me to respond to Evers's call for volunteers to stay after the meeting. He was seeking organizers to go into Jefferson Davis County and other areas where black disenfranchisement had been occurring. The job would entail organizing blacks to return to their county clerks' offices and re-register to vote, or register for the first time, as was more often needed.

This was a pivotal moment in my young life of seventeen years. Here was my chance to turn my thoughts and feelings about the need to improve conditions for blacks in Mississippi toward a specific action: in this case, fighting voter disenfranchisement. I reasoned that if anybody could do something about it, I could, and here was my chance.

The job would require me to confront the laws under which my worldview had been formed. The result would be a personal transformation so dynamic that neither I, nor Mississippi, would ever be the same again.

I did not go out seeking a "Cause." The Cause found me, placed itself at my feet, and said, "I'm all you got, boy, I'm yours." I decided that I was going to fight for the freedom of mankind.

Sometimes on Sunday afternoons, the black churches in Jackson would conduct "citizenship training," another method used to mobilize people in the struggle. At these meetings, Medgar Evers or another knowledgeable SNCC person would set the agenda for the coming weeks. Many such meetings were held. I remember one very well.

It took place on November 26, 1961. We selected committees to help blacks in the area pay their $2 poll tax. Various citizens of Jackson in attendance committed to recruiting 3,000 people for a Poll Tax march.

Other questions and mandates discussed at that meeting were as follows (from the printed agenda and my personal notes):

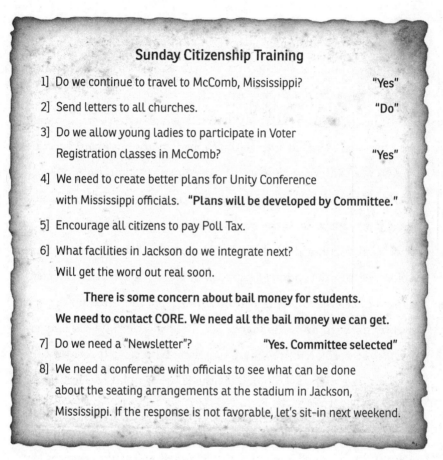

Sunday Citizenship Training

1] Do we continue to travel to McComb, Mississippi?   **"Yes"**

2] Send letters to all churches.   **"Do"**

3] Do we allow young ladies to participate in Voter
   Registration classes in McComb?   **"Yes"**

4] We need to create better plans for Unity Conference
   with Mississippi officials. **"Plans will be developed by Committee."**

5] Encourage all citizens to pay Poll Tax.

6] What facilities in Jackson do we integrate next?
   Will get the word out real soon.

   There is some concern about bail money for students.
   We need to contact CORE. We need all the bail money we can get.

7] Do we need a "Newsletter"?   **"Yes. Committee selected"**

8] We need a conference with officials to see what can be done
   about the seating arrangements at the stadium in Jackson,
   Mississippi. If the response is not favorable, let's sit-in next weekend.

The eligibility requirements for voting in Mississippi were among the most stringent in the South. In addition to a poll tax, there was a two-year residency requirement and a provision in the state constitution, referred to as the "understanding" clause, which stated a prospective voter must be able to read any section of the constitution, or as an alternative, be able to understand it when read to him, or give a "reasonable interpretation" of it.

As anti-black attitudes were then common, most county registrars, or circuit clerks, insisted that black applicants be able to read *and* interpret the constitution.

To help blacks counter this deterrent, I trained as a field worker, first with the NAACP, and later with the Congress of Racial Equality (CORE) and Student Nonviolent Coordinating Committee (SNCC).

At CORE, I worked under the directorship of Richard Haley, a field secretary. It was my understanding that Haley had been a music instructor at Florida A&M University for five years, and was released from that position because of his civil-rights activities. He would later be arrested in Jackson on July 19, 1961, for picketing a Southern Governor's conference.

Within each organization, my job was the same: to provide voter-registration training to blacks in the southern half of Mississippi, and get them to at least attempt to register to vote.

After my own short training session under the NAACP's leadership, I was assigned a rental car that had been leased by the organization and sent to southeast Mississippi. A fellow campaign worker would deliver the car to us. It worked that way with all of the civil rights organizations for which I volunteered, although sometimes we'd pick it up ourselves. What I could not understand, and really did not like, was the fact that some of the rental cars were the same make, model, and color, making them easy targets.

Medgar would make the decisions about who would be sent

where. Usually, he'd call the general number at Tougaloo and someone would relay the message. Students from Tougaloo and Jackson
State College also helped man his office and make phone calls.

Medgar would have already made the connection with a minister
or NAACP person in the community, had them set up a secret
location to hold classes, and start getting people to participate. The
ministers would sometimes announce during a service that a "voter
registration meeting" was going to be held at a particular time, and
encourage people to attend.

The other workers and I would then contact Medgar's lead person and arrange to gain access to the secret location. Blacks from all
walks of life, of different ages, education, and status would come to
the classes that were held after the work day.

Fear was prevalent. If word got out to the white business establishment, any one of the participants could lose his or her job, or
suffer worse.

Driving the lone highways through the Mississippi woods, you
didn't know if you were going to be stopped by the police or some
gang of idiots clamoring to beat you up or kill you. We took the
main roads as much as we could, but back in those days, there were
a lot of gravel roads in the rural areas where most of the blacks lived.

As the organizers, we would introduce ourselves at the meeting
and tell how and why we became interested in the freedom movement. We were there because we studied the history of the state,

and we knew the only thing that was going to change Mississippi was the vote.

We did believe it. The perception among those early participants was that their actions would help educate other black Mississippians and lead to change for the better.

Participants would sometimes lament abuses they had observed, or experienced themselves, in a culture that excluded them in every facet of society. Our response was to explain the registration process so they knew what to expect. We had to teach them the constitution of Mississippi because they would be tested on that.

"We will go and attempt to register," we'd tell them, "and more than likely, they won't let us, but we want them to refuse to allow us to vote, rather than do nothing and just say we couldn't vote."

Then, we would schedule a day to go to the courthouse. Sometimes I would drive them, or Medgar's lead person would. The whole group might go in at one time, or we'd stagger them, so one arrived about every five minutes. Other times, they would attempt to register without our help.

The result would always be the same: Registration would be denied. "You didn't pass the test" was usually the reason given, but no matter what answers black applicants gave, the circuit clerk would fail them. Our applicants would prepare to leave. The clerk, or other county workers present, would typically spout back anti-black insults: "Gon' on otta here antie. You need to be in da field. Do your boss know you're here? I'm gon' tell him now."

There were rare instances when one person might be allowed to register; that was more likely when movement workers were *not* present. However, the conservative political establishment was so dead set on not allowing us to succeed, they were more than likely turning away 99 percent of the people.

Those hardworking, law-abiding residents had one of the most despicable crimes committed against them. Their own state was denying them one of their basic rights, rights they were guaranteed as citizens born in this country.

Although I was only seventeen years old and not old enough to vote, I would, from time to time, attempt to do so. On one occasion, after I had completed the "Sworn Written Application for Registration," the circuit clerk just threw the form back at me. That wasn't bad. Some of the people were physically harassed, even beaten, for attempting to register to vote.

I had to ask myself, was I ready to accept the harassment? Was I ready to accept the beatings? Most of all, was I ready to accept death for my beliefs? I knew that I had already answered those questions in the affirmative. I knew that segregation was wrong and had to be stopped. I felt I had no other choice but to try to stop it.

A couple of us students at Tougaloo would sometimes leave for an assignment on a Saturday morning. When we returned on Sunday evening, the janitor would grant our request to lock us in the science lab, where we could study uninterrupted until the building reopened Monday morning. The janitors doubled as security guards. They were our friends.

I had many conversations with Medgar Evers about what was going on. He'd coach me on how I should present myself in various situations and with various types of people. He was never too busy to talk to me or anyone else. He taught me to be true to myself and to know who I was. He felt that if I wasn't "for real," it would surely come across in the form of mistrust. Most of all, he taught me that the civil rights struggle was not a game. It was a life-and-death struggle, and if I must die, then I should die with dignity while trying to help my people.

Sometimes, I called him, or he would ask me to come down to his office on the top floor of the black Masonic Temple in downtown Jackson to discuss a project, either one-on-one, or in a group. Other times, we talked on the phone. It was usually a reporting of how many classes, or how many had agreed to vote, and I'd let him know how many people I found willing to work with me, or who they were—if they agreed to reveal their identity.

As early organizers, we had few resources. We had no protection. On occasion, knowing full well that our small group was vulnerable to attacks by hateful mobs, I would ask for cover from law enforcement personnel, to no avail. The federal investigators, with their dark suits and skinny ties, stood out. None of us was opposed to walking up to them, particularly the FBI agents, and requesting their defense, even though the response was usually no.

If media personnel were at the public demonstrations that came later in Jackson, they often endured harassment and beatings, just as the civil rights workers did.

Even decades later, it's painful to speak of the experiences of my early civil rights years. I have to believe there must be something in a young man's DNA, something in his composition that steers him in the direction of a Medgar Evers. What is it that enables one to function while in the midst of such immense hatred? Somehow, somewhere, there has to be a blueprint deeply embedded in some of our souls that we are mandated to follow.

Some of my friends from the sixties and I get together occasionally. We ask ourselves why we created and participated in a particular protest. We don't really have an answer. Many situations were more than life-threatening. Some protests that we participated in were of such a nature that we were 100 percent certain that we would not survive. What made us do it? When a situation presented itself to us with a need to have our souls heard, we responded with sincerity. There was no hesitation. We not only participated "from the now," we participated from our souls. I would continue organizing black Mississippians to register to vote for the next four years.

On occasion, I shared voter registration training duties with white Yale and Bryn Mawr college students who had come to Mississippi to see "what the environment was like." This arrangement, quietly made by Medgar Evers, Tougaloo College, and the NAACP, was intended to send a message to the segregationists that we no longer would be intimidated, as blacks and poor whites usually were in Mississippi.

Two months before I finished high school, a black man by the name of Charles Mack Parker was arrested and charged with the rape of a young lady whose car malfunctioned on the highway near Lumberton, Mississippi. Lumberton is located less than seventy miles from my home, and news traveled fast. On April 24, 1960, Parker was taken from his Poplarville jail cell, beaten, murdered, and his body thrown into the Pearl River.

As a seventeen-year-old college freshman, I had the opportunity to take three Yale University students with me to Poplarville to help with voter registration classes. While driving west on Highway 26 toward our destination, I noticed the student sitting in the front seat with me had rolled down the window and extended his obviously white arm out for comfort. With a stern voice, I instructed him to place his arm back inside the window immediately! I explained that I did not want the opposition to see us sooner than necessary, and that I wanted to die after the meeting, not before the meeting. He had no idea what I meant.

We arrived at the prearranged meeting place only to find that it was not set up for class. When I inquired about this, I was told that the police had just left, and they had asked if any NAACP people had been there. People at the site no longer wanted the class to be conducted. I was reminded that only a few months earlier, on April 24, 1960, Charles Mack Parker was murdered in Poplarville. It was time to travel back to Jackson.

I had descended deep into the underbelly of Mississippi's decrepit soul. Like any man, I wanted to live to see the arrival of freedom for all, but I never expected to survive. This was the Mississippi that allowed lynching of its black people. The same Mississippi that allowed the lynching of black soldiers of World War I, some still wearing the uniforms they wore in battle while fighting to keep Mississippi Klansmen free to murder and create mayhem.

Sometimes I would call my mother and inform her of some of my travel plans for the weekends. I believe that she thought that I was "brave," but I believe that most of all she thought I was "right." Dad was a different story. He thought that I was right, but he also thought that I was reckless and asking for trouble. He thought that I had a death wish: "They will kill you, son!"

Years later, Joyce and Rose Parkman, two young ladies who were originally from our Lucas community, would visit my home in Illinois. Of course, their family knew my family well. They began to tell me how afraid my mother had been for me. That was the first time I had heard that. I had never known my mother to express fear concerning my civil rights organizing activities.

On some occasions, I was told by law enforcement officials to leave some of the small towns that I visited. Many times we were jeered at and threatened. I considered my state of Mississippi to be the most viciously racist in the United States, but because we believed in what we were doing, no threat or harm could stop us.

I knew that nonviolence was the only way for me. I had to make the segregationist understand that love is more powerful than hate. No matter what he did to me, I had to exert only passive resistance. I had to continue to show only love. I had to reach his "inner self" to show him that he was diminishing his self-worth by his actions.

As I walked through the shadows of hatred from others, I found strength and light in that old Negro spiritual by Thomas A. Dorsey, "Precious Lord, Take My Hand." My mother would sing that song after I'd relate to her one of my civil rights experiences. At times, when I thought that there was no way out, when I thought, "this might be my last day," I would walk with tears in my eyes, fear in my heart, and remember her singing the words to "Precious Lord, Take My Hand."

Some of my Caucasian brothers from the North who came to the aid of the foot soldiers fighting for freedom in Mississippi would tell you that nonviolence was being used in the South as a tactic. I submit to you that nonviolence was a way of life for black Southerners. It was not only a source of spiritual sustenance, but a method of survival. We knew that we were children of God. We knew we could prevail over persecution.

Use of the Ghandian mode of nonviolence as a tactic became increasingly prevalent in the movement. It was not difficult for most of us from the South to try to change the hearts and souls of the segregationists by following the path of nonviolent, passive resistance. We had been taught the art of passive resistance most of our lives.

Medgar Evers was one of the bravest men I have ever known. He did more for the state of Mississippi than anyone. After his tour of duty as a soldier in World War II, when he experienced a more tolerant, racially integrated society in Europe, he returned to Mississippi and the injustices of Jim Crow, and he became so angry he wouldn't stand for it anymore. Medgar fought tirelessly against discrimination in the laws and culture of the South; however, he rejected any use of violence as a means to improve our plight.

I would sometimes get tired of the organizers from the North who claimed to know how we blacks felt about our situation in Mississippi. Many organizers from the North thought that black Southerners felt that because they had been in the muck and mire of segregation for so long, they were "stuck," and that there was nothing that could be done. That is far from the correct analysis.

There were two completely different points of view among black Southerners when it came to speaking out against segregation. One segment of the black population told the organizers that they didn't "want to be bothered." This type of reaction was precipitated by fear. This was the segment that perhaps had more to lose if their association with the organizers became known—that job that held everything together and was the means of survival for themselves, their children, or other dependant family members. That position was not easily understood by some of our Northern organizers.

The other segment of the black population was willing to listen when approached by organizers. They had been looking for a leader or leaders. They wanted someone to provide some direction. As Jane Pittman said when the organizers approached in the movie *Miss Jane Pittman*, the people wondered: IS HE THE ONE? IS HE THE ONE?

Make no mistake: these two segments watched out for each other. The first segment would often say, "I've got your back" to the second segment. They often ran interference for the second segment. They often distracted the enemy away from their activist brothers. They provided a sometimes invisible and sometimes aggressive line of defense. One should never discount that first segment of blacks. They are partly the reason that the second group succeeded. They made us a part of their community. They "covered" for us, and what a job they did. I salute them.

The success of the civil rights movement would not have been possible without the heroic efforts of the ordinary black men and women of the South. These were the "Little People"—a term coined by Medgar Evers—who fought the actual battle. When I speak of the "Little People," I lift up the sharecroppers, tenant farmers, cleaning women and cooks, teachers and students, and small business people of the South. They are the foot soldiers who made history.

Most were not photographed, and their voices were seldom heard. They spoke not to the glare of television cameras, but to the hearts and souls of the black masses.

It was difficult for leaders to come up through the ranks of the "Little People," when they had all they could handle, just trying to stay alive. This was Mississippi, man! So this other segment said, "I'm willing to take a chance; I'm willing to listen. What is it that you as an organizer wish me to do?" And the answer was "We want you to stand up for what you believe is right. We want you to fight your best fight against segregation. We want you to be willing to die with us for the cause." These organizers often taught the Fannie Lou Hamers and others who developed into great leaders.

In 1960, black Mississippians were aware of the public protests taking part in other parts of the South. We were not yet ready to make that move; however, we were floating the idea of public protests at mass meetings. Medgar was worried that those tactics just might not work in Mississippi. He was concerned that we did not have enough legal and financial support in the state. There were very few black lawyers in Mississippi.

Another factor working against us was the *Jackson Advocate*, the largest black-owned newspaper in the state of Mississippi. Movement people thought founder and owner Percy Green was a black segregationist.

He was indeed a conservative black man. However, if one viewed his work only through the window of history, one might conclude that he was a racist segregationist; should by no means take away from Percy's original intentions for the newspaper, which was conceived to give a voice to oppressed people in Mississippi. Founded in 1938, the newspaper was the pride of the black community in the 1940s.

It was in the 1950s that Green lost the backing of most of the black community. During that time, he profusely criticized the efforts of black leaders. Later, Green printed editorials criticizing the efforts of the Freedom Riders: "Many (Negroes) have been heard to express the opinion that Negroes of the city (Jackson) would be better off if the Freedom Riders had never come to Jackson." Thirty-two Mississippi natives who would join the Freedom Ride proved that opinion to be wrong.

In addition, to the dismay of blacks, Percy Green began accepting money from the Sovereignty Commission, the state agency whose aim was to destroy the civil rights movement. Even Green's civil rights leadership in the 1940s and 1950s and his determination to make a contribution to the struggle of African Americans in the South was all overshadowed when he became critical of the movement. He allowed his newspaper to become a tool of the white segregationist power structure.

Because of the black newspaper's political position, in the spring of 1960, Medgar embarked on another tactical promotion

for the civil rights of blacks: economic boycotts. However, he felt
that the Jackson Negroes needed to be educated about what a boycott really meant. At various mass meetings, we began calling for
area students to join us in the education of the Mississippi Negro.
It was estimated that more than 600 students from various schools
and colleges showed up for duty. In early April, 1960, these students began visiting the homes of more than 5,000 blacks in the
city, informing each household of boycott, plans for an Easter week
and advising them not to shop at stores that discriminated against
them. Some of the blacks contacted were indeed pessimistic about
the boycott, and some were puzzled. It was as if we (the students)
had to tell them things that they knew so well. We had to remind
them that those were the same stores that would not let them try on
a pair shoes because they were Negroes. The same stores that would
not hire them or let them eat at the lunch counters located within
the stores. We had to remind them of the things that had been happening to them all their lives. Most blacks were ready to boycott and
wondered, "What took you so long to get here?"

The Easter week boycott (April 10 to 17, 1960) of Jackson's
downtown businesses was a huge success. Once we started, our
determination was that we would never turn back, even though
some blacks who continued to shop at the white-owned stores were
harassed by other blacks. On occasion, their purchased items were
taken and destroyed. Organizers never knew if they would return

home from these actions. When we planned them, we prepared ourselves to die.

Meanwhile, voter registration campaigns remained constant throughout the state. That summer, I was sent by the NAACP to many small towns in southern Mississippi to train and register black voters. I always thought if I remained in my home state after the summer of 1960, I would be killed.

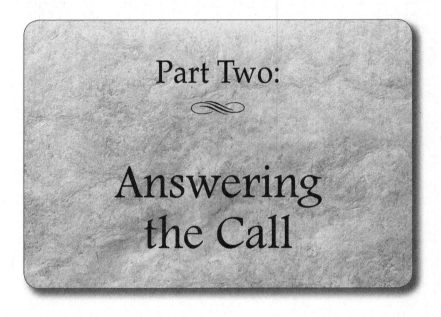

Part Two:

Answering
the Call

4

Cornerstone: Tougaloo

B EING PART OF THE struggle in the early days was somewhat different from the days after the Freedom Rides, when the movement gained greater momentum around the country. There was no national media coverage. While we were breaking the laws and customs of the South, we were viewed as troublemakers, if not criminals. It required "gut-wrenching courage," but we gladly participated in the picket lines and marches. We were there because we felt we had to be there.

Students at Tougaloo were somewhat isolated from the early visible action. I was relegated to voter registration and department-store protests. I was trying not to get arrested so I wouldn't cause Medgar any problems with the NAACP. The first activity to gain national attention was in Greensboro, North Carolina, at the first lunch counter sit-in at a Woolworth's department store, on February 1, 1960. Tougaloo students did not stage a sit-in until thirteen months later, in March of 1961. You may ponder why this was the case. My own determination is that it was because of a lack of aggressive leadership.

While various actions had been playing out for some time in Mississippi, they began to intensify after a group of Tougaloo students staged the first public demonstration.

On the morning of March 27, 1961, the "Tougaloo Nine," as they came to be known, stopped at the Carver Library, an all-black library, to request books they knew would be unavailable there. They then proceeded to the main library branch on State Street, where they looked through the card catalog, took books off the shelves, and sat at tables and read. When the police arrived, they ordered the students to the "black library." When the students refused to leave, they were arrested and held for more than thirty-two hours.

The names of the Tougaloo Nine were Ethel Sawyer, Meredith Anding, Jr., James Sam Bradford, Alfred Cook, Geraldine Edwards, Janice Jackson, Joseph Jackson Jr., Albert Lassiter, and Evelyn Pierce.

My grandmother,
Annie Armstrong

Me at twelve years old with Mother

My dad, Enoch Barnes

Millsaps College students protest the fatal police shooting of freedom demonstrator Ben Brown.

Deloris Dunlop was my classmate at Tougaloo.

Jan Hillegas, an organizer for the movement, at a civil rights and anti-Vietnam War protest in Jackson.

Strategy sessions were held every Friday night at Ed King's house (Ed is fourth from left) on Tougaloo's campus to plan demonstrations that would be held Saturday morning.

The Tougaloo Four, the first Mississippi Freedom Riders, were arrested June 23, 1961. With me (top left) were Mary Harrison, Elnora Price, and Joseph Ross.

Armstrong

Harrison

Freedom Riders Group Eighteen

Price

Ross

Rev. Ed King invited Northern ministers to join students in making interracial visits to local churches.

Some ministers came prepared to be arrested and taken to jail, like the minister in the foreground reading to (left to right) Julie Zaugg, Connie Shepherd, and Patsy Matthews.

Jimmy Travis, MacArthur Cotton, and me, all former Tougaloo students, reunited in 2008 at a Mississippi Civil Rights Veterans' Conference.

Dorie Ladner, like all of my friends from the movement, is like a member of my family.

Joan Trumpauer's senior portrait from high school.

My wife Jeannette and I have been together since 1968.

In later years, Ethel Sawyer and I corresponded, and she reflected on the experience: "The Tougaloo Nine struck a major blow to the prevailing attitudes held by European Americans in the state of Mississippi that all were in agreement on the appropriate "place" of African Americans. The blow sent shock waves throughout Mississippi's collective and individual systems. When the nine Tougaloo College students walked into the Jackson Municipal Library on March 27, 1961, in what is referred to as Mississippi's first sit-in demonstration, the state of Mississippi would never again be the same."

The arrests of the Tougaloo Nine prompted students at Jackson State College, the larger, local black college funded by the state, to organize a public vigil. Joyce and Dorie Ladner were among students expelled for participating in the demonstration. Administrators at their school would not condone anything that might be construed as a challenge to the laws of the state, in the interests of its standing with the government of Mississippi.

The sisters transferred to Tougaloo, and joined our "band of brothers," as Dorie liked to refer to our group of freedom demonstrators. Often, when speaking with Joyce, I got the impression that their reason for choosing Tougaloo was because of its involvement in the struggle. Many of us at Tougaloo wanted to be a part of that library sit-in, and after it happened, the school's chaplain, Edwin King, a young white Episcopal minister, and Medgar Evers became less restrained in their leadership, allowing our demonstrations to pick up momentum. They called for action, and more students in addition to those who had already been involved in protests responded—ready, willing, and able to work to finish the job.

The start of the student sit-ins alerted the rest of the nation to the growing resistance to segregation in the South. The sit-ins attracted the interest of professionals and students in education, politics, law, and religion, who would travel South to get involved.

Out of Harlem, New York, came Bob Moses, a talented mathematician, teacher, and graduate student of philosophy at Harvard University. His goal was to take the life out of segregation in the Deep South by going for its heart. He went to Atlanta first to work with SNCC, but Ella Baker and others there convinced him that to accomplish his task, he needed to organize the grassroots—the small farmers, sharecroppers, and day laborers in Mississippi.

Moses made the trip to Jackson, where he met Medgar, who sent him to work with Amzie Moore, an NAACP organizer in the Delta. The largest numbers of black Mississippians lived in that section because economic opportunity was richest, but the exploitation of blacks was so egregious that they were forced to live in third world conditions.

Moore convinced Moses that the key to breaking the grip of segregation would be the vote. Moses found a typewriter and hammered out a voter registration project that won SNCC's approval. He started in the Delta, but eventually moved his base of operation to McComb, where he worked with local movement leader Curtis Bryant. There he opened a Freedom School, teaching the state constitution and mobilizing blacks to get registered.

On the occasional weekend at Tougaloo, when I took the bus home to Prentiss, which was about thirty miles southeast, I had to make a choice: Either ride at the front of the bus and risk getting arrested, or ride at the back. At first, I sat in the back with the rest of our folk. But the freedom movement had been enlightening. I knew that I didn't have to accept second best, and other Negroes weren't putting up with it, either. Medgar had instructed me not to get arrested unless it was sanctioned by the NAACP; however, I was determined to not sit at the back of any bus.

This created a dilemma. How could I exercise my part in the movement while not getting arrested? First, I would always try to be one of the first ones on the bus; if the third seat from the front was available, I would sit there. Sometimes, the driver would insist that I "move to the rear of the bus." When that happened, I would sit as close as possible to the front, behind the cloth curtain that separated the blacks from the whites. The curtain was hanging on a rail and you could move it. When the driver wasn't looking, I'd move the curtain forward one seat and then move myself up.

Most of the time, the driver was the same person on that route, and he didn't care where I sat. It was when a white person was on board the bus and saw me sitting up front that the driver would demand I move. At that point, if I didn't move, he would call the police. Never once did another black come to my aid during the times I decided to oppose being moved to the rear. Once, a small, elderly black lady spoke up and said, "Son, we don't want no trouble, just come on back here, and sit with us."

Before I moved away from Lucas to go to college, I would often question my mother about the Emmett Till murder. All she would say was, "We have to make things better."

Her statement was not the reason I had now joined the movement, but it became my leaning post.

Many people doubted what I was trying to do. Some thought that I was being silly and foolish, or even crazy. Nonviolent resistance was not on their agenda. However, it took little persuasion to get them to realize that something needed to be done to improve our living conditions.

You must understand that Southern segregationists truly believed that black Mississippians were happy. My goal was to somehow show them that their assessment of "black Mississippi life" was beyond unreasonable. Lord, just let me live long enough.

In the struggle for freedom in Mississippi, Tougaloo College was the mother that rocked the cradle. Any and all steps toward justice in the Magnolia State can be attributed in part, if not fully, to Tougaloo students and staff such as Chaplain Ed King. He worked with the NAACP to organize students for demonstrations, including the first public sit-in, driving civic activism in the state to a new level.

Tougaloo was a special place. It nurtured the inquisitiveness of one's soul. The faculty had the difficult task of instilling the college's philosophy of the independence needed to function in a segregated society into the minds of poor, undereducated black students. We learned that "now" was the time to affect change.

Tougaloo was a beacon shining on all dark corners of a segregated Mississippi, and it was that light that was used by many of the foot soldiers to courageously navigate the dangerous roadways of hatred. While sitting on the grass under the old moss-draped oak trees on campus, planning the next protest with other schoolmates, we felt that we could change the world.

Tougaloo Eagle Queen

TOUGALOO, EAGLE QUEEN, WE LOVE THEE,
MOTHER EAGLE, STIR THY NEST.
ROUT THINE EAGLETS TO THE BREEZES,
THEY ENJOY THE TEST.

That verse of my Alma Mater almost always brings me to tears. It has more and more meaning to me as time goes on.

We always had special guests to visit the campus. One of them I remember well—Bob Zimmerman, better known today as Bob Dylan.

Below is an e-mail message that I sent to a few movement friends after seeing Bob's 2005 film, *No Direction Home*, directed by Martin Scorsese.

Sent: Wednesday, September 28, 2005 12:09 AM

Subject: Bob Dylan—*No Direction Home*—Film

Hello Dorie, Joan, and Joyce:

I must say that I have a different perspective of Bob Dylan now than what I had of him during our conversations in Mississippi in 1960. At that time, I thought that Dylan showed empathy for the civil rights movement. He saw the emotion. He expressed the understanding. He had the ability to come to the civil rights scene, digest it, and put together some of the greatest "protest" songs ever. His way of manipulating words got your attention. His "story," even though he may say that there wasn't one, changed one's way of thinking. I know that he was in "constant movement" within his music. Even Joan Baez could not slow his musical movement or change his direction. He had a musical mission. Bob had something to say, and he said it in a way that others wanted to but couldn't.

Bob always had the ability to bounce back. He could show us that there was still something left in him. The material was great. Bob is an icon. Bob's demeanor in the last segment of the movie (just before his accident in real life), indicates that a type of demise was taking shape. Yet, I think he overcame it.

There was a kind of mystique about Bob. His guard was mostly up at all times. He did not want you inside his head. If you inquired of Bob "who are you?" Bob would want to know why you are asking such a question. To him, it was as if you were indicating that he was more than who "Bob Dylan" was. He did, however, spend a few days in the Mississippi Delta visiting one of the Freedom schools. The school students really enjoyed those music sessions.

Upon viewing the film No Direction Home, *I see that Bob had no empathy for the movement. He had absolutely no control over what direction he or his music took. He was destined to write and sing the songs that he sang, but he never wished to try to change the world with his music. He just wanted to sing. Home, unknowingly to Bob, was in his music. There is no direction to the present. Similarly, he will forever seek a new home. When he reaches his new home, those of us left will continue to marvel at his journey. I salute Bob Dylan.*

Thomas

As I stated above, "He had the ability to come to the civil rights scene, digest it and put together some of the greatest 'protest' songs ever." He would tell you that he didn't write "protest songs." He would tell you that he was not a "folk singer." As he stated in 1965 in a *Time* magazine interview, "I don't have anything to say about the things I write. I just write them. There is no great message."

Many of us who met Bob Dylan in the South thought that he might one day become a spokesman for the movement. We were wrong. He was not, in our sense of the word, a freedom fighter. Bob was a poet: a great poet.

Yet, ask yourself this question: Why did Bob Dylan teach a music class in the Ruleville, Mississippi Freedom School in 1964? Of this freedom school highlight, Margaret Block (freedom fighter), stated that, "It was so cute, how he would gather the children around him and then play the guitar and sing with them." (Where Rebels Roost: Mississippi Civil Rights Revisited) That's the Bob Dylan we knew in 1960.

One beautiful night in April 1964, in Tougaloo's Woodworth Chapel, Joan Baez drew what was at that time the largest completely integrated audience ever in the history of Mississippi. Because of the efforts of Tougaloo chaplains John Mangum and Ed King, the chapel can be considered the place of origin of Mississippi's civil rights movement, along with the Masonic Temple, where Medgar had his office.

During the tumultuous 1960s and early 1970s, speakers and entertainers who performed in the chapel included such icons as Ralph Bunche, Julian Bond, Stokely Carmichael, James Baldwin,

Roy Wilkins, Martin Luther King, Jr., Medgar Evers, Robert F. Kennedy, Fannie Lou Hamer, Harry Belafonte, Leontyne Price, Frank Sinatra, Andrew Young, Bayard Rustin, James Farmer, Jr., James Forman, James Baldwin, Marlon Brando, Sammy Davis, Jr., Burt Lancaster, Dick Gregory, Joan Baez, and many others.

The L. Zenobia Coleman Library at Tougaloo maintains a vast collection of documents, tapes, and artifacts related to the movement, along with the personal papers of many Mississippi activists. Notable alumni of the college include Walter Turnbull, the founder of the Boys Choir of Harlem.

5

Becoming a Freedom Rider

O N MAY 4, 1961, AN INTERRACIAL group of thirteen activists, organized by the Congress of Racial Equality (CORE), boarded buses at the terminal in Washington, D.C., and rode South together. They split into two groups—some rode on a Greyhound bus, the others on Trailways.

Their destination was New Orleans, requiring travel through six states: Virginia, North and South Carolina, Georgia, Alabama, and Mississippi.

Intent on ending racial segregation in interstate travel, the group was embarking on a *Freedom Ride*—a tactic of *nonviolent direct action*, the strategy pioneered by members of CORE. National director James Farmer had been among members of the civil rights organization who had organized a similar demonstration in 1947, called the Journey of Reconciliation, the model for the 1961 Freedom Ride. CORE's Washington staff recruited and trained the new of group Riders, seeking to raise the pressure on the federal government to end segregation in the South.

There should have been no question about racial segregation in interstate bus travel. The Supreme Court had twice declared it to be an unconstitutional violation of human rights. Also, the Interstate Commerce Commission had banned race restrictions on buses and trains, lunch counters in terminals and airports, and in restrooms.

Nevertheless, in 1961, interstate travel was still segregated. Conflict between certain states and the federal government over enforcing civil rights protection blocked any possibility of change.

The Freedom Riders knew that Southern segregationists could be counted on to violate their civil rights, and that their simple acts of defiance might very well cost them their lives. However, they were undeterred in their efforts to force an apathetic nation to see the inequality they exposed and test the will of the administration of President John F. Kennedy to resolve it.

Many of these men and women were beaten, bombed, harassed

and imprisoned, but, as historian Ray Arsenault declared in his book *Freedom Riders* (2007), collectively they turned a pivotal corner in the Civil Rights Movement and demonstrated the power of individual action to transform the nation.

On the whole, what started out as a single Freedom Ride in the spring of 1961 had, six months later, evolved into a full-scale movement, with more than 400 Americans—young and old, male and female, black, white, religious and secular, from the north, south, east, and west—riding integrated Freedom buses into the Deep South.

In the security conscious, Cold War suspicion of that era, most Americans thought of the Freedom Riders as promoting social disorder, given to reckless abandon, and would-be martyrs.

A national Gallup poll, conducted late in May of 1961 after the Rides started, found that 60 percent of Americans agreed with the Supreme Court's ruling that racial segregation on buses and trains was unconstitutional. However, only 24 percent agreed with the tactic of the Freedom Rides.

Most of the Freedom Riders were ordinary people, many of them college students, as well as clergymen of various faiths and labor leaders. CORE recruited them from a network of civil rights organizations with wide-ranging concerns, from war and poverty to voting rights and social intolerance. Each was required to sign an application consenting to participate, and they received some prior training. They were encouraged to think of themselves as role models. Farmer imposed a strict dress code: coats and ties for men, dresses and high heels for women.

Their courage and unbending optimism produced a series of actions that shocked the nation into seeing, up close, the unresolved human crisis that propped up segregation.

On May 14th, Mother's Day 1961, two weeks after the Freedom Ride embarked on its journey, the Greyhound bus carrying Riders and regular passengers pulled into a deserted terminal in Anniston, Alabama. The bus was surrounded by a screaming mob of about fifty men and boys, some of whom were later identified as Ku Klux Klansmen, carrying metal pipes and chains. The passengers had been able to seal the door for a time.

Unable to get inside, the mob began a series of attacks on the exterior of the bus, breaking windows and slashing tires. The crippled bus returned to the highway, where the swarm of vigilantes returned and firebombed the bus. The passengers barely escaped being burned alive. Some were beaten as they came off the bus. As they sat on the ground, coughing and bleeding, a crowd of white residents from the surrounding community mostly stood by and watched, except for a few, including a twelve-year-old girl who carried buckets of water to aid the injured. The girl's family was later run out of town for her choice of action, as I understand it.

That same day, one hour after the Greyhound bus first pulled into

Anniston, the Trailways coach carrying Freedom Riders also reached Anniston, where a mob boarded the bus and beat the Riders with fists and clubs. The bus managed to escape Anniston and reach Birmingham, where the Commissioner of Public Safety, "Bull" Connor, encouraged another mob to savagely attack the Riders a second time, leaving them bloody and battered.

That evening, in the lobby of a dormitory on Tougaloo's campus, I sat with other students, riveted to the television news broadcast of the savage scene: the flames that consumed the Greyhound bus and clouds of black smoke rose into the sky, the beaten and, bandaged Freedom Riders both black and white, who would not be stopped. It had an enormous impact on my life.

The Kennedy Administration's lack of concrete support for the Riders to this point helped to solidify my adherence to the movement. I felt that I had to do something to help gain that critical presidential support.

Civil rights protection went to the very core of Tougaloo's historic tradition. The courage of the Freedom Riders touched the hearts and minds of everyone there. Students followed that first Ride with great intensity. As the demonstration continued, we would gather around various television sets in the recreational and other common areas on the campus after classes and lunch each day.

We were anxious to absorb whatever information came in about what was happening to the brave men and women who had come from all over the country and were our same age.

The Freedom Ride almost ended after the attack in Birmingham, until a second group of students, mostly from the Nashville sit-ins, came in to replace the first group. The FBI, meanwhile, provided no protection for the Riders.

The second wave of Riders left Birmingham on May 15. At the terminal in Montgomery, they too were viciously attacked as they stepped off the bus. Several were chased into the streets and into other buildings as they sought cover. Somehow they managed to get back on the bus and continue their ride. The next stop would be in Jackson, Mississippi.

For what had seemed like a month leading up to this point, as if expecting an invasion, officials in our state began what I call the The Big Lie. They wanted the world to think that they intended to treat the arriving Freedom Riders with the greatest amount of professionalism and courtesy. The unspoken truth was they thought they would teach the Riders a lesson.

"Mississippi is ready," declared John Wright, head of the White Citizens' Council in Jackson. At the same time, other officials were said to be informing the U.S. Justice Department that all the Freedom Riders would be killed if they came to Mississippi. As a student body at Tougaloo, we were not going to let that happen without a fight.

That same night, Governor Ross Barnett appeared on TV telling everyone, "The Nigras in Mississippi are satisfied with the conditions here." That made me furious. I rejected the idea that the lives of black Mississippians should be confined to second-class citizenship.

Witnessing the horrific attacks on the Riders made me realize I had to get more deeply involved in the freedom struggle. I had to let the world know that most citizens of Mississippi were tired of being at the bottom of the economic and education ladders. Blacks were tired of inferior schools and housing conditions. We were tired of not being able to make enough money to feed our children. I wanted to send a message to Governor Barnett: "You are wrong in your assessment of the black citizens of Mississippi."

First Freedom Ride Arrives in Mississippi

The first group of Freedom Riders arrived at the bus station in Jackson on June 2, where they were met by a horde of policemen. There was no violence, though we at Tougaloo felt the Riders were not safe. In a ironic twist, two of the police dogs used by the Jackson Police Department, Happy and Rebel, were trained by Harry Nawroth of Springfield, Missouri, the former Nazi storm trooper who trained killer Dobermans to guard Adolph Hitler's airports. As soon as the Riders stepped off the bus and walked into the bus station, crossing the color line in the waiting room, they were almost immediately arrested and carted off to local jails.

Students at Tougaloo were taking in all of these events as we continued our classes with crossed fingers and hopeful hearts. One of our prayers was "let the Riders survive their stay in jail."

A small group of us, maybe ten or twelve, kept track of the number of Riders who had been injured and taken to hospitals along the way, and we checked regularly for details about their whereabouts. We knew that we were expecting twenty-seven Freedom Riders; therefore we wanted to make sure that twenty-seven arrived in Jackson. We were glued to radio and television for any type of information we could get on them. We were prepared to take action to help them.

Shortly after the Freedom Riders had been booked into jail in Jackson, they appeared in court. They were quickly found guilty of "breach of peace," and sentenced to sixty days in the state's maximum-security prison, known as Parchman Farm, Mississippi's ultimate humiliation. The prison houses death row inmates and is located on a 21,000-acre farm.

CORE called for other civil rights organizations to support a "jail-no-bail" initiative, aimed to fill all of the jails in Mississippi. That's when hundreds of people from around the country began to board buses bound for Jackson. After the first group of Riders were arrested and jailed in Mississippi, another group came in, then another, and another. By the end of November, as many as 406 Freedom Riders had come into the state,

Almost daily, the newspapers ran editorials and politicians made speeches claiming, "All the trouble in Mississippi is being caused by outside agitators." They ignored the fact that there were Freedom

Riders who were native-born Mississippians. The segregation fathers had overlooked the June 2, 1961 arrest of Leslie Word, a black male Freedom Rider from Corinth, Mississippi, because he came into Jackson on the freedom bus from Montgomery. The arrest on May 24, 1961 of James Bevel, a CORE activist born in Itta Bena, Mississippi, did not count. Bevel was considered an outsider, since he was a student attending American Baptist Theological Seminary in Nashville.

Those of us who had been engaging in acts of protest in Mississippi were eager to start a larger movement of our own. However, the reality was that we did not have a plan. Our NAACP base had limited legal counsel and money for bail bonds to support the numbers of people who would be required to risk arrest. We were filled with hope and anticipation as CORE and SNCC began to accelerate the movement for civil rights, taking it out of the courtroom and into the streets.

The 1961 Freedom Rides formed the backdrop to a dramatic interplay among CORE, SNCC, the NAACP, state and federal government, the press, and the public. These interactions brought ideas, power, courage, and unity to the movement, while accentuating the conflicts that would eventually sunder the fragile alliance of civil rights organizations.

It is true that the NAACP did not particularly care for the Freedom Rider tactic. But even so, one NAACP officer did not always adhere to all of her organization's policies. When Ella Baker felt that the NAACP's methods were taking too long to produce results, she and her followers decided another organization was needed. They wanted to develop an organization that was deeply rooted in religion and free to take independent action against a segregated system. Thus, the Southern Christian Leadership Conference, SCLC, was formed.

Similarly, Ella determined that the role of young people needed to be defined within the framework of SCLC. It was decided that yet another organization, specifically for youth, was needed. To implement and lead the new organization, James Lawson, who had been associated with The Fellowship of Reconciliation and a member of CORE, was chosen. He had already been conducting nonviolent workshops at Vanderbilt University in Nashville. His new trainees included Bernard Lafayette, Marion Barry, James Bevel, Diane Nash, John Lewis, and others who became the "Nashville Group"— The Student Nonviolent Coordinating Committee, SNCC.

Tougaloo Four Leads
Mississippi Freedom Riders

SNCC leaders James Bevel and Bernard Lafayette, both original Freedom Riders, were released soon after their arrest in Jackson. They came over to our campus to organize a meeting for recruiting people to continue the Rides to New Orleans. I had met Bevel earlier that day, and I helped set up the meeting. We had discussed the training and possibility of my joining the Rides. Later at the meeting, when Bevel called for volunteers to continue the Rides, I spoke of my desire to support the effort and of the need for "Mississippi Freedom Riders." Then Bevel asked me, "Well, what are you going to do about it? Will you volunteer to become a Freedom Rider?" I agreed. I found it amazing that only two Tougaloo students volunteered straight away: Mary Harrison, a twenty-one-year-old Asian American from San Antonio, Texas and myself, then a nineteen-year-old sophomore. But we wouldn't be alone for long.

6

⧉

In the Stillness of
the Midnight

THE FREEDOM RIDE WAS scheduled to continue from Jackson to New Orleans on June 23, 1961, which would include a stop in McComb, Mississippi. No other students had volunteered to join the ride, so we thought it would be only Mary and me on a bus leaving Mississippi. She and I began to fill out applications to join the rides and firm up our plans to meet at the Trailways Bus Station in Jackson.

To become a Freedom Rider, one had to make the higher-level commitment to nonviolent direct action—which was viewed within the state of Mississippi as irresponsible and possibly suicidal. By signing on for the demonstration, we agreed, too, with CORE's position—that federal law was on our side, and that to test enforcement of the law, we would refuse to be segregated on an interstate bus. We were picked up on the morning of June 23 by Mrs. A. M. E. Logan, who drove us within a block of the bus station on Pascagoula Street in Jackson. Mrs. Logan knew our anxiety was very high. Mary and I did not know what fate had in store for us. We mentioned it was possible that we would be beaten or killed.

Elnora Ross Price and Joseph Ross, siblings from nearby Raymond, Mississippi, would join Mary and me on the first local Freedom Ride. Joe Ross was a visiting student from Tennessee State University and had helped train Freedom Riders in Nashville.

Mrs. Logan, a Jackson resident, had risked her life daily by transporting civil rights workers from one place to another, often receiving harassment and threats. She did all she could to keep us calm and, at the same time, raise our spirits.

As the four of us—Elnora, Joe, Mary, and me—departed the automobile one-half block from the Jackson bus station, there were no policemen in sight; however, their presence soon became evident as we walked up to the entrance.

We walked in, purchased our tickets to New Orleans, and proceeded to the waiting room designated for whites. Upon crossing that color line, we were met by Captain J. L. Ray, Chief of Police for

Jackson, along with a horde of policemen. Three times, Captain Ray informed us that we should leave, because we were disturbing the peace. Three times we informed him that we wanted to board the bus for New Orleans, adding at one point that if he looked around, he would note the people inside the station were all smiling. The white bystanders were grinning at us being treated like criminals by the gang of police.

We had simply walked into the bus station and acted as though segregation no longer existed. That warranted our immediate arrest. The police escorted us out of the building and into separate paddy wagons to be transported to jail. The Freedom Ride would not be allowed to continue out of Mississippi, but other measures would be taken to keep the nonviolent, direct-action protest against segregation going into New Orleans.

The Freedom Rides evoked suspicion and outright hostility from white Southerners, and many different people in the South and throughout the country. As the first residents of Mississippi to join the Freedom Rides and get arrested, the local papers branded us as the "Tougaloo Four." Dozens of other black Mississippians would also join the Rides.

In the small town environment in which I was raised, getting arrested for anything brought shame on both a person and his or her family. I had to overcome that way of thinking and show others the difference between "Just" and "Unjust" laws. We were standing up and breaking unjust laws that had been put in place solely to dehumanize blacks. We felt it was of critical importance to defend our beliefs and to support the collective effort to bring about the liberation of all.

Inside the paddy wagon that I occupied was a person who appeared to be homeless. When the driver accelerated quickly, both of us would slide to the rear of the vehicle. Then, if he applied his brakes forcefully, we would slide to the front. This went on until we reached the Jackson City Jail. The other guy never said one word.

At the Jackson City Jail, I was fingerprinted and interrogated. The officers wanted to know who forced me to enter the bus station against my will. I told them I was there to prove that Governor Barnett was a liar. There were a lot of other questions, such as who paid for the bus ticket, who transported me to the station from Tougaloo College, and was I a Communist. I responded to every question with a question, and that infuriated them.

I was placed in a cell with a white man who appeared to be the same street person who had been in the paddy wagon with me. The clanging sound of those large jail doors closing was unforgettable. The food brought to me was unfit to eat, and I refused it. Then, there was the anxiety of being locked up in a cell with an unknown person who had unknown intentions. As in the paddy wagon, I had an instinct that warned me that I was being set up to react a certain, unfavorable way; therefore, I did not speak with my cellmate that day.

Late on the night of June 23, I was transported to the Hinds County Jail, where I was placed in an empty cell. Once again, the sound of the closing of those large, steel doors was horrible. I believe that isolation was designed as a method of harassment.

As I sat there in that jail cell, I began to wonder if I had done enough. Was I making a difference? Deep inside, I felt that I had, and I was. And then, from deep within the bowels of that facility came the mighty sounds of people singing, "We Shall Overcome." Peace came riding in like a hurricane. I knew there were Freedom Riders near me, but not in my sight. At night, I could hear them singing freedom songs. I couldn't carry a tune, but I would sing as loud as I could. Inside those walls, I felt freedom.

Around midmorning on June 24, I was taken again to an inter-rogation room. This time, the ordeal was a little more intense. After I had given the officers basic identification information, I refused to provide any additional information. I knew there was no such thing as being read my rights, or being allowed to call an attorney. This was Mississippi. When I arrived back at my cell, the songs began again. Even though I was not in the immediate area of the other freedom fighters, I was on the same floor as they were. We sang freedom songs all day.

Among the hundreds of Freedom Riders starting to pour into Mississippi from around the country was Mary Hamilton, now deceased. She was a person of color who looked white. She was from Cedar Rapids, Iowa, and was teaching English at a Los Angeles parochial school when she decided to join the Rides. She was booked into the Jackson City Jail on June 25, 1961, while I was there. I did not see her, but she met the two female Mississippians with whom I had been arrested, and wrote of the experience in a journal. A friend of Hamilton's recently posted excerpts online:

From "Freedom Riders Speak for Themselves," by
Mary Hamilton, of Los Angeles, arrested and jailed in
Jackson, Mississippi, June 25, 1961

At the entrance to the Jackson City Jail, there is an inscription that says this building was erected for and by the people of Jackson, Mississippi, in honor of liberty, equality, and justice—or something like that. Everyone who saw it commented on our state of liberty and equality.

We entered the jail and were taken to the office. Our personal things and bags were then taken from us. We lined up one by one and had to empty everything from our purses.

The official who checked our money and belongings had put on my slip that I was white. When the girl behind me told me, I notified him otherwise. He was very angry. He told me that I was lying, and that I'd better not try to fool them. I told him I wasn't lying or trying to fool them, and would he please change the identification. He did this after conferring with two other plainclothesmen, but he was obviously disturbed. *This also happened to the other girl. By this time, we were getting a big kick out it.*

Then we were lined up to be fingerprinted and photographed. When I went in, I was told to be seated and asked if I had any scars. I told the policeman, "No." He asked me if I was sure, so I said, "None that I can recall."

He then looked at my face, around my neck, through my hair, and at my arms. He discovered a scar on my elbow, and told the typist to write it down. He asked if I had any others, and I said, "No."

After that he said, "Are you a Negro?"

I said, "Yes."

He said, "What else are you?"

I said, "I'm Negro and nothing else that I know of."

He then took it upon himself to decide what other races I could be, and told the typist to put down that I am Negro, white, Mexican, and I believe that's all. That made me very angry, because I felt he had no right to take it on himself to decide what race anyone could possibly be.

He told me to get up. I was fingerprinted. Then I was taken to another room where all the family history was taken down. After that, we were taken into a room that was locked. When all the four Negro girls were finished, we were taken to a cell. There were two other Freedom Riders already in there. We were very surprised to see them, and very happy.

These two girls were students from Tougaloo College, which is just outside of Jackson, Mississippi. One was from Texas, the other from Jackson. After we introduced ourselves, they told us that they and two fellows from Tougaloo had decided to go on a Freedom Ride to refute Governor Barnett's public declaration that all Negroes in Mississippi are satisfied. These four were only the first from Mississippi to go on the Freedom Ride.

Also in our cell were four other Negro women inmates. We introduced ourselves and told them we were Freedom Riders. While they didn't speak much, their manner was very friendly. Before we left, we gave them our Freedom Rider buttons, which they took very gladly, and concealed.

On each side of us there were women inmates. As we sang our songs, or shouted down the corridor, or across the way to get to other Freedom Riders, the other inmates said, "We know who you are, Freedom Riders. We're with you. When we get out, we're going to join you."

Sunday, June 25, was a day of rest, relaxation, and reflection. Only once did I ask myself the question: "What am I doing here?" I knew why I was there. Among other things, I was there because I wanted the State of Mississippi to obey federal laws as mandated by the United States Supreme Court. I was there because I wanted Governor Ross Barnett to understand that all people of Mississippi were not satisfied with the living conditions in our state. I was there because too many of my family members, as well as other Blacks, were unlawfully deleted from the voter registration rolls in 1956. Yes, I was there, locked up in that jail cell because I wanted to be there.

On the morning of June 26, 1961, my third day in jail, I was taken for an initial court hearing, which was filled with testimony from policemen complaining of both my attempts to incite violence and the ugly demeanor of the people in the Trailways bus terminal. My testimony indicated that "everyone in the terminal was smiling, except the policemen who were present." I was found guilty, sentenced to four months in jail, and fined two hundred dollars.

I spent only a short time in the Hinds County jail and avoided going to the Parchman Prison Farm. After three days behind bars, something unusual happened. The president of Tougaloo College, Dr. A. D. Beittel, who was a supporter of the freedom movement, bailed me out. That was shocking, since I was prepared to spend a minimum of forty days and a maximum of six months in prison, in keeping with CORE's jail-no-bail tactic.

By early July, an influx of thirty-two black Mississippians—including more students from Tougaloo, Jackson State College, and Jackson area high schools—had followed the lead of the Tougaloo Four. Most of the Freedom Riders arrived and were arrested at the

Jackson, Mississippi bus terminals in groups. The now defunct Mississippi State Sovereignty Commission classified the riders according to the group in which they were arrested. The state would later classify them as Freedom Rider Group Eighteen. The actions of the Mississippi Freedom Riders mobilized the greatest amount of local support for the freedom struggle, which helped to dispel the notion that black Southerners were too beat down or were complacent, and reinforced the reality that organized resistance had become a fact of life. Various other civil rights activities were initiated in the state.

Black activists born and raised in the South accounted for six of the original thirteen Freedom Riders and approximately 40 percent of the four-hundred-plus Freedom Riders who later joined the movement, according to historian Ray Arsenault.

"The Freedom Rider movement was as interregional as it was interracial," Arsenault wrote, "though in the public consciousness, the typical rider was an idealistic white activist from the North or an older religious leader. It did not seem to register with people then, or even now, that black Southerners were actively involved."

The Freedom Rides shook up the white establishment all over the state of Mississippi. On July 3, 1961, nine days after I arrested, state officials began using an all-out smear tactic against the Freedom Riders. T. B. Birdsong of the Mississippi Highway Patrol stated that the Freedom Rides were directed, inspired, and planned by known Communists. A pawn in this game was Katherine Pleune, a twenty-one-year-old Freedom Rider who had visited Cuba on a "Fair Play for Cuba" tour the prior winter with 201 other students. Birdsong's charges produced a denial from a New York official of CORE.

Although CORE was calling for support of its Jail-No-Bail tactic, Freedom Riders Elizabeth Adler and Peter Ackerberg did not adhere to that request, and appealed their cases on September 5, 1961, as did Zev Aelony on September 6, 1961. Expensive appeal bonds were threatening the financial solvency of CORE. On September 6, 1961, Freedom Rider Alex Anderson tried to withdraw his appeal, but he was not allowed to do so, thereby further draining the resources of CORE when they had to pay his bond.

On the morning of September 8, 1961, Attorney Jack Young counseled his client, student Frank Ashford of Marion College in Chicago, to plead *nolo contendere*. For doing so, Ashford received a suspended sentence of four months in jail and a two-hundred-dollar fine.

On the afternoon of September 8, 1961, my appeal was heard. Standing before Judge Moore, I used a different tactic. I plead not guilty. Apparently, the judge did not appreciate that, and sentenced me to the higher penalty of four months in jail with release on a fifteen-hundred-dollar bond and a two-hundred-dollar fine. Because I was known as a committed organizer in the movement, the NAACP paid my bond.

After my case was heard, CORE's officers instructed their lawyers to counsel their clients to plead *nolo contendere* at their trials.

My case took on greater significance when merged with a larger federal class action lawsuit, Bailey v. Patterson, filed by NAACP attorneys.

Upon my release, the attorneys began preparing me to testify in the federal court case, which was heard in Jackson that summer. The attorneys, including Bill Kuntsler and Constance Baker Motley, required me to stay in Jackson, rather than go home to Lucas, so that I would be readily available when called to take the stand.

The class action case that would later become the U.S. Supreme Court case *Bailey et al. v. Patterson et al., 369 U.S. 31 (1962)* had been originally filed on behalf of Joseph Broadwater, former president of the Jackson NAACP, Burnett L. Jacobs, an active NAACP member, and Samuel Bailey, vice president of the Jackson NAACP. My case and two others involving Doris Ruth Bracey and Medgar Evers were included.

Doris Ruth Bracey had been arrested when she sat at the front of a local Jackson bus and refused to move after police asked her to do so. Medgar Evers testified in the class action case that on March 11, 1958, he boarded and sat on the front seat of a Continental Trailways bus in Meridian, Mississippi. He was arrested when he refused to move to the rear after he was asked to do so by a policeman. This class action sought to enjoin the city of Jackson and the state of Mississippi from continued arrest of interstate, as well as intrastate, passengers. It was filed by NAACP attorney Constance Baker Motley, and on federal appeal, opened the way for public transportation on a nonsegregated basis in the state.

The suit claimed the plaintiffs' right to desegregated transportation service, and accused Mississippi of failing to uphold desegregation laws as dictated by the Interstate Commerce Commission. We were denied by the state, and on appeal to the federal district court, "pending construction of the challenged laws."

The NAACP sought relief directly from the U.S. Supreme Court which, on February 26, 1962, vacated and remanded the case back to the U.S. District Court for the state of Mississippi for "expeditious disposition," stating:

> ". . . as passengers using the segregated transportation facilities, they (appellants) have standing to enforce their rights to nonsegregated treatment," and ". . . that no State may require racial segregation of interstate or intrastate transportation facilities has been so well settled that it is foreclosed as a litigable issue."

In the messy unraveling of segregation laws in Mississippi, we eventually won our case the following year.

Parchman, Joan, and Beyond

Teams of Freedom Riders continued to come in and fill up the jails in Mississippi in September. At Parchman, they were forbidden cigarettes, shoes, reading material, and exercise. They were issued T-shirts and shorts that didn't fit. Except for a few minutes for supervised shaving and showering on Mondays and Thursdays, they were kept in their cells around the clock. The lights were kept on all night, which made sleeping difficult. Sometimes at night, fans were turned on and windows opened, which, inside the prison's thick walls, made it very cold inside. When they sang freedom songs, their mattresses would be taken away. They were not allowed to associate with anyone except their cellmates.

Hunger strikes occurred among Freedom Riders in Parchman. Price Chatham, twenty-nine years old, from Long Island, New York, fasted for twenty-four days without food and drank only water.

The first group of Freedom Riders began to be released from Parchman in late July and early August, 1961. Some of them stayed on in Mississippi to support other civil rights actions, including registering blacks to vote. A few of them enrolled at Tougaloo.

When classes resumed in the fall of that year, several of my new friends were Freedom Riders and others in the struggle. Joan Trumpauer was among them.

Joan was living in Washington, D.C., when she joined the Freedom Rides. She grew up in Arlington, Virginia, but most of her family had been raised in the Deep South. She would refer to most of her relatives as "old-line Georgia." I recently asked her to think back to her decision to engage in civil rights action and share her insights. From Joan in her own words:

My mother's side of the family was your stereotypical Georgia red-neck (that's the only way I can put it), Pentecostal. I think that exposed me to a lot of the rural Deep South, hearing them express their attitudes and religious fervor. My father's side of the family was more college-bred Iowa. My folks had met in Washington, D.C., during the Depression. Though my closest identification was with the Georgia branch, I also had this relationship with the other side of the family. My Iowa family cancelled out my Georgia family.

My involvement came about from my religious conviction and the contradiction between life in America with what was being taught in Sunday school. I was at Duke University in Durham, which was the second city to have sit-ins, and the Presbyterian chaplain there arranged for the students from North Carolina College (NCC), to come over and talk with us about what the sit-ins were about and the philosophical and religious underpinnings. We had to keep pretty quiet because you could be locked out of the buildings, or burned out, or any number of things on campus. At the end, they invited us to join them on sit-ins in the next week or so, and that started a snowball effect.

Duke and I became incompatible over this, and I dropped out and was working in Washington, D.C., actually in Senator Engels's office, involved with a group called NAG [Nonviolent Action Group]. Hank

Thomas was going on the Freedom Rides, and we thought this was a big joke and gave the poor guy a hard time, thinking he was off on this cushy all-expense-paid vacation because exams were over; but we quit laughing when the bus was attacked and burned in Anniston.

People from my group, Paul Dietrich and John Moody, were going down to Montgomery, and my apartment had a direct off-campus phone that was a clearinghouse for the Washington, D.C. people who joined the Freedom Rides.

By the time I went, things were rolling a bit, and we flew to New Orleans with Stokely Carmichael; I like to say that I brought him to Mississippi. We flew to New Orleans and had a little orientation there, then took the train in. We got arrested. The part that really sticks in my mind was I was 110 pounds with curly blonde hair, very Southern-looking, and after they arrested me, stepping out of the paddy wagon at the jail, and the police officer reaching out to help me down the high step, and saying, "We don't want anything to happen to you, little lady," and then catching himself and realizing he was being a southern gentleman, and I was a Freedom Rider. This horror struck withdrawal on his part. So, it was two months and I think a two-hundred-dollar fine in my sentencing.

Since I had already been accepted at Tougaloo, I would serve the two months and work off the fine until time for school to start and pay the rest. So with the clothes on my back, I enrolled at Tougaloo.

Acknowledging the injustice and the need for civil rights action in Mississippi brought forth in me—and many other people—extraordinary courage. I went from typical teenager to crusader for change in society.

Throughout the remainder of 1961, I continued as a field worker for SNCC and CORE. Some of my duties were to:

1. organize and carry out protest demonstrations
2. assist in voter registration drives
3. obtain police protection for Freedom Riders, who were heading into and out of Mississippi

These were responsibilities that I did not take lightly.

I became fast friends with MacArthur Cotton, a fellow brother, who was tall, husky, and born in Kosciusko. He had just come into Tougaloo as a freshman, and straight away put himself in the freedom movement. I admired that. In late November 1961, CORE and its supporters were still trying to resume the Freedom Rides from Jackson into New Orleans. The last leg of the trip required a stop in McComb, Mississippi.

On November 30, MacArthur and I were asked by Thomas Gaither, field secretary for CORE, to travel to McComb to meet a group of six Freedom Riders who were scheduled to arrive there the following morning from Baton Rouge, Louisiana. The names of those six were: Thomas Peete, Patricia Tate, Jean Thompson, Claude Reese, Lillie Bradford, and George Raymond. George Raymond had been arrested August 13, 1961, at the Trailways terminal in Jackson.

What happened next would outplay our worst fears. It illumi-
nated the raw hate that we knew some of our fellow Mississippians
had for black people, and we wondered if we would ever be able to
change how they felt or the way they had been taught to treat us.

McComb was among several Mississippi cities that filed state
injunctions instructing the Greyhound Bus Company to maintain
segregation signs at its terminals. In McComb, however, Greyhound
painted over the signs. Once that was done, the city of McComb
erected new signs that read "White Waiting Room—Intrastate Passengers." The U.S. Justice Department then filed an injunction
against the city of McComb on November 2, 1961, claiming that
its enforcement of segregation could cause the Greyhound terminal
to close and the company to lose employees. The signs eventually
came down, but not for a couple of years.

On Wednesday, November 29, two days before MacArthur and
I met with the interracial group of Freedom Riders who were en
route from Baton Rouge, five Riders arrived in McComb from New
Orleans. They were Alice Thompson, Doreathea Smith, George
Raymond Jr., Thomas L. Valentine, and Jerome Smith. They were
beaten by four white men at the Greyhound Bus Terminal. Of
course, help from local law enforcement personnel was late arriving.

The following day, the State Sovereignty Commission dispatched
A. L. Hopkins to McComb to investigate the matter and to offer

assistance to local police and city officials. Local authorities refused the state's assistance.

McComb's Police Chief George Guy informed state investigator Hopkins that there were "several FBI agents and representatives of the U.S. Justice Department in McComb," according to Sovereignty Commission files. Investigator Hopkins reported to his office that there were approximately twelve FBI agents and between two and four Justice Department representatives believed to be assistant United States attorneys general. Hopkins also reported that several newspaper, radio, and television reporters and cameramen from many sections of the country had come to McComb to photograph and report on matters there.

Newspapers reported the arrival of the Freedom Riders that day in McComb, stating that a mob of approximately four hundred people greeted them by shouting profanities all at the same time, with Police Chief George Guy safely hidden away in a nearby billiard parlor.

From my personal notes of 1961:

12:55 PM:

On the afternoon of December 1, 1961, MacArthur Cotton and I arrived in McComb, Mississippi, at approximately 1:00 PM driving two cars, one of them a red four-door 1961 Chevrolet. (Those of us working with CORE and SNCC often pooled our resources, and it was not unusual for vehicles to be loaned or borrowed.) We parked the automobiles one block from the station. The streets immediately surrounding the station had been closed to traffic. We proceeded on foot toward the police station.

I spoke with the assistant police chief, who informed me that we could not come and "take over their town," and that I could not park there. He then asked me, "Do you want to drive this thing, boy, or do you want me to drive it?" I moved the car a half-block from the terminal. Mac moved his car.

After parking our cars farther back, we walked to a street corner where several police officers were standing. I spoke with the officers concerning how deserted the streets were. One officer remarked that the street was now closed. Again we proceeded toward the police station. We were met on the street by the chief of police, George Guy.

1:15 PM:

I met with Police Chief George Guy, who asked what time the Freedom Riders would be leaving the terminal after they arrived. I told him that it would be about fifteen minutes after arrival. I inquired as to his protection plans. He stated that he would escort us to the railroad tracks. I walked to the bus terminal for inspection. As I proceeded to the bus terminal, I recognized an FBI agent. I explained to him that I expected the arrival of six Freedom Riders and was requesting his protection. I was informed by the agent that all he could do was record what happens. I requested that he keep his "eyes open." I recognized the agent, because I had seen him at other protest demonstrations. I could only see a few people in the bus terminal.

MacArthur and I could not risk entering the "White Only" station at that time. The Police would surely arrest us if we did so. The assistant police chief and I crossed paths again. He requested that when I respond to him I do so with the words "Yes Sir." I couldn't afford to get arrested at that point in time. Other officers approached us.

I was asked to produce my ID. I presented my selective service card and driver's license to the heavy officer standing next to me. I had forgotten that I had two selective service cards in my wallet. Lucky for me, I had taken out the old 1–A card and not the new 1–Y card. I had informed the selective service board that I would not be participating in the military service. I gave as a reason an old injury. Upon examination by the military doctor, I was reclassified as 1–Y.

The policeman recorded the information he wanted from the cards and returned them. He had misspelled my hometown. I was then told that I could not come back to "this corner." The police volunteered to escort MacArthur Cotton and me to the railroad tracks. I informed the assistant chief that we were expecting the arrival of six Freedom Riders on the next bus, and that we would appreciate any assistance he could provide. Specifically, we would like police protection when leaving the terminal. He did not reply.

1:33 PM:

*The Bus was now arriving. One, two, three, four, five, six: Six Free-
dom Riders entered the "White Only" waiting room. Coworker MacArthur Cotton entered terminal to meet Freedom Riders and to escort
them to our car located a half a block from the terminal. I was standing with the assistant police chief and a tall lanky police officer who
was cleaning his fingernail with a long switchblade knife (between car
and street corner). The assistant chief went across street to the City Billiard Parlor. He enterd and closed the parlor doors, leaving only two or
three policemen in the street.*

1:38 PM:

*Sensing trouble, I felt that I had to go and get the Freedom Riders
and MacArthur Cotton out of the terminal (no one would ever know
how they died in there). Nor would the world know how I had died out
there on the street. At this point I didn't know that there were newsmen
at the corner from the station.*

1:40 PM:

*After informing the Freedom Riders of the situation outside, we
prepared to depart the waiting area. As we open the door to exit
the "White Only" waiting room, the door to the City Billiard Parlor
opened and more than fifty people exited. People began coming out*

of all the nearby buildings. One half of the city block was filled with people. They all rushed toward us with sticks, paper bags, filled socks, and other items. They were shouting many curse words. Along with unrepeatable words they were calling us names like Rabble Rousers, Communist crackpots, agitators, and G–D Niggers. It appeared as if they were possessed with demons. I can even now close my eyes and see demonic images spewing from their mouths.

The usual mob rhetoric was directed toward the group: We were surrounded. There was plenty of cursing, name calling, pushing, and shoving. MacArthur Cotton was struck on the knee by a segregation-ist, with a sock filled with some unknown item. Even while being bat-tered, we managed to somehow make it to the two cars. A lot of news reporters were standing in front of Hollis's Drive Inn. Some were being attacked. MacArthur and I were dragging Freedom Riders, who had been knocked down, to the cars and shoving them inside. We managed to get in, start the cars, and begin moving. I knew that the police were there, but I didn't see any. I slowly drove through the riot seeking a path to accelerate out of there.

We made our way to a predetermined safe house in McComb that was owned by Mrs. Willie Mae Cotton (no relation to MacAr-thur Cotton). While there, we received death threats via telephone. Carloads of unknown people cruised by. We didn't feel safe there. In other words, we felt less safe there than in most places in McComb.

There were noises outside—sounds of objects hitting the house. "Was that a brick being thrown at the house?" Windows were knocked out. Some of us slept under beds that night.

As a last-minute alarm, I placed a Coca-Cola bottle on top of the door handle, then obtained a dishpan from Mrs. Cotton and placed it on the floor under the door knob. If anyone shook the door, threw a brick against the door, or turned the door handle, the bottle would fall in the pan and awaken everyone.

At one point the next day, December 2, 1961, MacArthur stated he thought we would never leave McComb alive. One of the amazing things about that experience is that MacArthur and I had survived. We were both certain, and expecting, that we would not. The following year the home of Mrs. Willie Mae Cotton was bombed.

The next morning, Sunday, December 3, friends of ours drove the Freedom Riders to Brookhaven, Mississippi, where they boarded the bus and traveled to Jackson. MacArthur and I visited a McComb church and rallied the people to get out and vote and integrate all of the local facilities.

After speaking at the church, MacArthur and I went to the train station attempting to catch a train out of McComb, but the train operated on an odd schedule. We went back to the church. The word was out that "outside agitators" were operating in McComb. The police department and other "concerned citizens" were searching for us. Deep in our hearts, we just knew that we were near the end of our lives. We were in the "stillness of the midnight." Would Jesus understand?

At the beginning of the Sunday night church service, one of our local acquaintances, knowing that we needed to leave town, told us that he could get an automobile. A few minutes later, he drove up in a car and motioned for us to get in. He drove us to the Brookhaven bus terminal.

During the drive, he told us that he had hot-wired the automobile of one of the church mothers who was attending church service. He had to return it before service was adjourned. In case he did not return in time, he promised us that he would drive the car to the church and tell the owner what had happened. We arrived approximately thirty minutes prior to the departure of a bus that would travel past Jackson, Mississippi. Separately, we purchased tickets to Jackson and boarded the empty bus parked in the dark parking lot.

Thinking that this might be our last night on earth, we placed our fingerprints on all the windows of the bus. We were hopeful that if we were killed, perhaps someone would find the prints and know, through this gesture, that at least we did get on that bus.

We did some serious thinking while waiting for that bus to depart. I thought, *Will I ever see my parents again? Maybe, these being my last moments, am I as committed to the cause as I thought I was?* I was thinking about one of my mother's predictions: "Your [birth] mother was a Christian, therefore nothing is going to happen to you." I wondered if the prediction would hold true this time. Mac would only say, "My friend, we will know soon enough. Now let's get some sleep."

MacArthur Cotton and I knew that McComb was a "hellhole of racist activity." We just didn't know how much. That city's black communities suffered no fewer than sixteen bomb attacks by vicious, racist, American-hating people in the early sixties.

It was not until 1964 that the "Colored" and "White Only" signs came down in McComb, when a three-judge federal appeals court panel ruled Mississippi's segregation laws unconstitutional.

On the ride back to Tougaloo College, Mac and I sat at the front of the bus without incident. We arrived in the early morning hours, just in time to shower, glance at our assignments, and go to class. No one in class knew what we had just lived through. The next weekend, we participated in a sit-in at a restaurant in Jackson.

I've seen my black and white brothers and sisters beaten and bombed, simply because they wanted improved conditions for the people of the state of Mississippi. I have walked through mobs of hate-spewing demigods who were pushing, shoving, and hitting demonstrators. Yet, I have never received more than a push from a white racist. I always said that it was because of my mother that I was never attacked.

Repression, not violence, was directed against me. It's repression when schools are not equal, when blacks cannot live in places they can afford. It's repression when blacks can't get loans and jobs to purchase homes and start businesses, when blacks are the last hired and the first fired. It's repression when blacks can't get proper medical care. It's repression when black Americans are excluded from first-class citizenship.

7

Friends of
the Spirit

RIDING IN A CAR ALONG the major highways through Mississippi, whether in the front seat, or the back, Negroes always had to be on guard.

The experience was not unlike being under constant threat of attack, whether it was the indignation of having to relieve oneself on the side of the road because public restrooms at gas stations were not open to blacks, or the insecurity of pulling up to the bumper of a pickup truck that had a shotgun lying in the back window.

As more people became aware of the growing Mississippi non-violence movement in the wake of the Freedom Rides, our group of student activists at Tougaloo started mobilizing larger numbers of black voters.

Actively working for social change wasn't something you did to "be cool," Dorie Ladner recalled when I saw her last year at a civil rights veterans' conference in Mississippi. "It wasn't a party," Dorie said, "It was a commitment." With other veterans and college students, she sat on a panel about the state of young people engaged in work for social change.

"We were like zealots," she said. "We used to say 'put your body in the movement.' Once you got into it, you were in it. You couldn't just be there and say I'm going to sing, and not get involved."

"People would try to *kill* you," she said with emphasis on the "kill," and paused to sit up in her chair. "We were a threat to their (white Mississippians) way of life."

Dorie and her sister, Joyce, grew up in a small black community south of Hattiesburg, called Palmer's Crossing. They had come to know Medgar Evers from their experience volunteering with the NAACP Youth in that area. Their engagement in SNCC was actually death-defying. The Ladner sisters were arrested many times for their movement activities.

For several years prior to the Freedom Rides, white individuals from various parts of the nation, some from foreign countries, had already been journeying into Mississippi to teach in the black colleges as part of an organized opposition to segregation. Many were tormented by law enforcement, but they never wavered from their commitment.

At the same time, students from Millsaps, the all-white Methodist school in Jackson, would sometimes join in protests or stage demonstrations of their own.

Millsaps students occasionally joined our group of student activists at Tougaloo in what became known as "strategy sessions." The meetings were held in the campus home of Chaplain Ed King and his wife Jeanette. Some of the whites, especially those from the Jackson area, had never sat in a room with black people their own age. As a precaution, Ed always kept a bright porch light on as people arrived. It was necessary in those times for anyone opening the door to see clearly who was knocking.

There were times when Ed and Jeanette would bring a particular racist problem to our attention, and then leave it up to us as to how we would handle things. There would be times when the Kings, or some of the rest of us, felt that a particular demonstration would be too dangerous. Our question to Ed would then become, is it really necessary that we protest this issue? Of course, that was a question we had to answer personally. However, things were made much easier by friends like Peter Stoner, who would invariably say that we had no choice. We had to go. At that point, we knew that he was right.

Pete, a white male from Pennsylvania, came to Mississippi as a Freedom Rider from Montgomery, Alabama on July 2, 1961. He remained in the state and participated in voter registration campaigns. He enrolled at Tougaloo, where he volunteered for many civil rights projects.

Pete was arrested June 2, 1962 for picketing in front of the Federal Building in Jackson. It is said that he once went to the local jail to see Lawrence Guyot, who had been arrested in a demonstration. Guyot was one of the lead organizers from the Mississippi Gulf Coast, and had come to work in the Jackson movement. He would later become chairman of the Freedom Democratic Party. Because he was not allowed to see Guyot in the jail, Pete protested so vehemently that he himself was arrested.

I knew Pete as a person who wanted to be where the action was. Whenever a protest was taking place, or even if it was just in the process of being planned, Pete was ready to go—*now*. He worked in many small towns in the Mississippi Delta. He remains a loyal soldier for freedom in the state of Mississippi and lives in Jackson.

In November 1961, I started to become better acquainted with Joan Trumpauer, the young lady who'd come to Mississippi as a Freedom Rider and told me her relatives were "Old-line Georgia." (Joan generously shared her own retrospective on why she chose to involve herself in the struggle for racial justice in the previous chapter.) Joan was friendlier than Charlotte Phillips, a bookish transfer student from Swarthmore College near Philadelphia who was from New Jersey, and Patsy Matthews, a bouncy, happy-go-lucky young lady from Wisconsin who smoked cigarettes. Prior to the enrollment of Pete, Joan, Charlotte, and Patsy, the only white students who had attended Tougaloo College were the children of white teachers.

Joan and I were close. We would speak to each other for hours on campus about any subject on earth. As she spoke to me, it was as if I could see her looking into the sphere of a better world. She spoke of a world that she wanted to see exist. She spoke of freedom and love, not just for my folks, but for her folks as well.

She spoke of her concern about why the world in general, and especially Mississippi, in particular, were not already better places. It was these long conversations that forced me to look within my being and ask, *Why do I feel the way I do? Is what I feel inside what I should feel inside? Is there room for change?* Joan helped place a shining light on some long-needed answers. The word equality now had a clearer meaning.

During many of our long talks, Joan appeared to express the belief that nonviolence and passive resistance were secondary components of the movement. She felt that these principles were somehow not interwoven with the greatest bond, and that compassion was the glue that held the movement together. She honestly believed that all the movement people had developed some kind of extreme humbleness and love for humanity. My expression to her was always that non-violence and passive resistance were not, for me, just a tactic, but a way of life.

At the expense of her own well-being, Joan was always trying to help someone else. After starting a family, Joan worked in the Arlington, Virginia elementary schools for thirty years. She wanted to make sure that her young students started life with respect for all humankind.

Our relationship was not about physical encounters. We both had an agape kind of unconditional love for family and mankind. We knew that we were on a journey. Where that journey would lead us, we did not know, but we knew that the journey would not allow us to be complacent. Because of our true agape love, we were forever bound, and we knew that it was not our words that mattered. It was our attitude and what was in our hearts that mattered. Our interests were being directed by the teachings and spirit of Jehovah.

Of course, there were times when I was ridiculed by members of my own race because of my perceived relationship with Joan. Those were very, very depressing moments, because I knew that I was right, but on the other hand I thought that I understood the feelings of those who disapproved of that perceived relationship. During those very trying times, it was Joan's thoughtfulness and strong support that pulled me through. No, no one, not even Joan, will ever understand the importance of her being in my life during those times.

Some at Tougaloo said: "Why are you so friendly with Joan and members of the other races?" I believe that it was not a matter of my being "so friendly" with Joan and members of the other races, but those relationships were so overt to others that they sometimes saw it as improper. It was my way of dealing with all people without bias. I think that I did that, and I'm proud of it.

Being proud of my treatment of different races may be attributed to my family and training. My grandmother was of Caucasian heritage. Also, after the first semester of my freshman year of college, one of my roommates was always a foreigner, including Ng Yan Kit of Hong Kong, Dindial Mahabir of India, Fitz Waithe of Paraiso, Canal Zone, and Peter Wong of Hong Kong. I think that to a certain extent, a role was being played in my relationships with my foreign fellow students at Tougaloo College. I saw them as individuals who were there to help. Because of this, I wanted to do all I could to protect them and to make them feel comfortable. But I was most closely associated with Joan Trumpauer because, to me, she was a lot more than just a white person at a black college. She was there because of her philosophy and her commitment. Joan was not there to just gain friendship, but to make a difference, and she did. She made a difference.

Joan was for real, and I loved her for that. She never allowed her whiteness to overshadow relationships. In dealing with her, I never flaunted blackness. Our relationship was one of cold reality, so yes, we were both pricked by the pins of the perception of life as it had been taught to us, but we knew what we wanted this world to be—a beacon of truth.

In the movement, Joan Harris Nelson Trumpauer was my best friend. To this day, she indeed remains my friend. She will always be my hero.

Later that fall of 1961, I went home to Lucas one weekend.

I can remember telling my mother about my new friend Joan and her commitment to the struggle, and to mankind in general. Mother was distraught. I could just see her mind racing back in time as she cried: "Oh, Lord! Son, what are you about to do? Please don't get involved. Don't you realize where you are? These white folks will never let you and your friend stay here. You bring her here and they will kill you deader than a doornail."

I could see her hurt in her eyes. I could even see the hurt that her mother went through, loving mankind while living among people who attempted to lynch her husband, my grandfather.

Of course I was already in the hot seat with the Mississippi White Citizens Council and the Ku Klux Klan in southern Mississippi. My family and I knew that "certain people" were trying to find me, and if they did, I would not live to see another day, especially if they found me in the company of a white woman. I had to make hard choices, although, really, the choice had already been made for me.

Dad was quick to back Mother up, saying: "Please don't bring your friend here, because the white folks are aware of your activities, so please don't put her in that situation. Don't put yourself in that situation. I want you to leave this place. They could kill everybody here, including your mother and me."

I couldn't leave. "I just can't," I told them, to which Mother insisted, "Yes, you can. If you stay here, they will kill you. Dad is right. They could kill all of us."

And Dad gave the final decree: "Don't bring that girl here and keep your own visits short, or we could all pay the price for your presence."

I felt the world was coming to an end. *What is it that my parents were asking me to do?* The thought of something happening to my best friend and my parents was overwhelming. The more I thought about it, the more I needed a drink.

My wiser choice, however, was to take care not to be easily spotted, and instead of taking the bus back to school, I drove my father's pickup truck. About a month or so later, I was returning home with the truck and decided to stop at the gas station nearby for fuel before continuing on home. I pulled into the station where one of my cousins worked, and I proceeded to pump fuel. It was the same gas station where my father and uncle purchased fuel for their log trucks and paid for it on Saturdays. After filling up, I went inside to pay.

As I entered the station, I could see several white guys and my cousin sitting around talking. My cousin was sitting in a chair apart from the group. The owner of the station proceeded to get up and walk behind the counter. Once he saw who I was, he told me I didn't have to pay, because he knew that my father would be there the following morning to pay for fuel purchased for the log trucks. I thanked him and turned to walk out.

As I walked away, my cousin spoke up and asked, "Thomas, that couldn't have been you that got beat up on the steps of the courthouse in Jackson this week, could it? You look just fine."

In fact, it was just that week, on Wednesday, December 4, 1961, that a gentleman named Thomas Armstrong was beaten. The story in the *Jackson Clarion-Ledger* on the following day reported that G. W. Hydrick, a white Hinds County bootlegger, pistol-whipped a photographer named Thomas Armstrong at a demonstration on the steps of the courthouse in Jackson. I explained to my cousin that while I had not been the one beaten, I had been there to see it happen. Friends put the other Thomas, who was bleeding profusely, in a car and rushed him to the hospital.

All the other men in the gas station began to join the conversation about what they had read in the newspapers that week about all the demonstrations going on in Mississippi. I don't know if the owner ever caught on to the reason I lowered my voice at that point, but when I gave my cousin the full name of the guy who was beaten,

I said it softly, hoping others would not hear. Maybe my prayers were answered, since one of the white guys asked, "Are you Enoch's son?"

"Yes, I'm Enoch *Barnes's* son" I replied, and walked out, trying not to arouse suspicion. I knew that the men in that gas station only needed to get my real last name and I would be in big trouble. After all, it was well discussed in the community that most of the whites in Silver Creek were Klansmen. It was said that the Klan reached all the way into the Mississippi legislature. One guy particularly mentioned was Silver Creek's Billy Joe Lee, a white segregationist.

There were two things that shielded me from the clutches of the segregationists. One was the fact that my last name was Armstrong and the last name of "my parents" was Barnes. Second was the fact that a somewhat well-known black photographer named Thomas Armstrong and I had the same name.

The segregationists in Silver Creek were confused. They had been notified that there was someone in their area of the country who was involved in the struggle. When they first began to zero in on me, I was directly confronted by several of the local whites, who asked if I was involved in particular situations that were occurring in Jackson, Mississippi. I lied and said, "No, it was the photographer." Even at that, I knew that they were getting close.

A few weekends later, I risked coming home again. A cousin, Paul Taylor, and I went to the town of Monticello, Mississippi, to see other relatives and friends. They lived, of course, in the black section known as "Peyton Town." I was inside my friends' home when one of the guys I knew from the neighborhood came running in. He announced that there were two carloads of whites who had driven down the block and were asking if anyone knew me and if I was in the area. My cousins thought that Paul and I shouldn't stick around and should travel the back route to our homes. Fortunately, the harassers did not return, and we were able to proceed home safely.

Now I knew for a certainty that the segregationists were on to me. After I pulled into Paul's driveway, we sat for a while, discussing the events of the night. Eventually, Paul got out, and as I was about to head home myself, he leaned into the car window and softly said, "I think you should leave this place."

He was no doubt right, just as I knew that my decision to take part in the movement was the correct thing to do. Segregation was wrong, pure and simple. It was wrong because it allowed people to hate. And there is no place for hate in a just and right society.

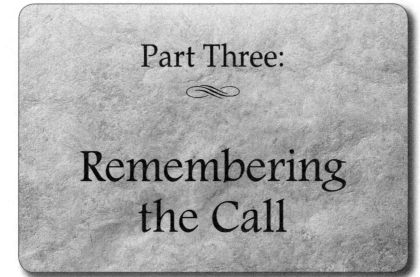

Part Three:

Remembering
the Call

8

Disillusioned

I NEVER WANTED TO SEVER TIES WITH my friends and family. However, both my mother and father were saying that I should leave, and there was one particular event that played a major role in them trying to push me out the door. As I mentioned earlier, my dad had a Caucasian friend in Silver Creek, Mississippi who was privy to major local Klan decisions. He notified us that the Klan had determined my identity.

When Dad came to me and said that it was time for me to leave Mississippi—now—he knew what he was saying. My cover was blown, the Klan now knew who I was, and the threats had begun. Threatening telephone calls in the middle of the night to my parents were not something I took lightly. It was a sad thing to have to watch my mother deal with them. It was because of my actions that my parents had to endure such hatefulness.

Therefore, after a few, short tearful conversations with a couple of close friends, I decided to leave Mississippi, even though I was just one semester shy of college graduation. It was January, 1962, and I only informed two friends of my destination: Kansas City, Missouri. My family and I had decided that I would first go to Kansas City, because the white Citizens Council would not expect me to go there. I purposely indicated to most people that I was destined for Chicago, because that is where I wanted the Klan to think I was going.

Two of my half sisters lived in Kansas City, so I lived with one of them. On several occasions, two white men unknown to us appeared at my door asking if a Thomas Armstrong lived there.

The answer was, "Who?"

Still, they persisted. I had no way of knowing that the long arm of the Mississippi State Sovereignty Commission (name unknown at that time) could reach all the way to Kansas City.

In Missouri, I was no longer with my known "community" of activists. I was no longer with very close friends. I was not satisfied with the "new group." I located the Kansas City chapter of CORE and began hanging out with them. Their movement was dull; I left them after a couple of months. I could not go home. My whole world changed. Depression set in.

I began my stay in Kansas City by living with my sister Kathleen. She was a nurse at the University of Kansas Hospital. Her husband, Marcus Tucker, was an entrepreneur. He was also a high-ranking member of the Prince Hall Masons. My other brother-in-law, Nevall Mitchell, was working at Fred Harvey Restaurant and asked me to work there as a fry cook. A cousin of my brother-in-law, Joseph, also worked there. I took the job and rented a bedroom in the home of an elderly couple located two blocks from my sister on Benton Blvd.

The landlord's son was a rail post office clerk with the United States Postal Service. He worked Wednesdays, Thursdays, Fridays, and Saturdays. Those were the kind of hours that I liked. Little did I know that several years later, I would have a similar job.

At night I would often wake up in a cold sweat, screaming, and the kind owner of the home would try to calm me. On one such occasion, I was dreaming that a hand was caressing my chest. I felt the hand and decided that it was the hand of a friend of mine. I touched her hair, only to realize it was too thick to be hers. I panicked. A group of people began kicking, beating, and cutting me, and there was a long gash across my chest. Frantically, I tried to get away. At that point I awakened and scrambled quickly out of the room. Luckily, I still had on my pajamas. The owner of the house had company, and there I stood in the middle of their group, bleeding and frightened to death. There was skin under my fingernails. In my sleep, I had scratched that hard across my own chest.

Both of my brothers-in-law were heavy drinkers, and as I sank farther into depression, the temptation to consume alcohol was too great. I began frequenting the bars around 19th and Vine streets; this was the worst part of the city. At that point, I was in a bottomless pit of nothing and was well on my way to becoming a functioning alcoholic.

The streets were filled with drunks, and each night fights broke out. I could feel that things were not right. A part of me knew I needed to leave before I was embedded too deep.

One night after leaving a bar, I was walking along the sidewalk with another person from the street. That person struck me with some object. Lucky for me, I was next to a boarded-up street-level window. I fell against it and into the window-well of an abandoned building. There was no pain. I pretended to be dead. The guy was afraid to go down the darkened steps into the lower level and soon left the scene.

A few weeks later, I was walking home around 1:00 AM. Intoxicated, I was surrounded by a group of guys who said they wanted to sell a pistol. I demanded to see it. I quickly noticed there was only one bullet in the revolver. I pointed it in the air and pulled the trigger. I was immediately struck on the head, robbed, and thrown in the bushes, out of sight. The robbery did bother me. However, what bothered me more was the fact that those young black men were now going to have a police record that would follow them for the rest of their lives. I would later discover that two of those lives were not long ones. One young man was killed at about the age of twenty-three and the other one died when he was near thirty years old of a then-unknown disease to be later recognized as AIDS.

Shortly after arriving in Kansas City, I met Regina Pitchlyn. Knowing her was good for me. She had a lot to do with my beginning the long, lonely ascent out of the gutter. I fell in love with Regina. She had two wonderful and beautiful children. They reminded me of how my birth father married my birth mother and was an instant father of seven children before having me. All seven of them grew to love him dearly.

While working the evening shift at Fred Harvey's Restaurant, I would get home late at night and very tired. Trying to impose some structure on myself, I wanted to get up no later than 8:00 in the morning. As Regina left for work she would board the 7:30 AM bus one-half block from where I lived. Often she would walk that one-half block and awaken me. She was such an angel, it was a wonder she didn't have wings.

Regina was responsible for what little sanity I had left while living in Kansas City. I came close to asking her to marry me but I was afraid that I might not be the kind of father that her two children needed. I knew that in my condition as an alcoholic, those children would be better off if their mother raised them as a single parent than with me around. Regina was a brave and beautiful young lady, and she would have no trouble finding someone more fit than I was to be a father. Once I made that determination, I knew that it was now time for me to make a difficult decision. I had to get out of her life, and I had to do it quick.

I was in the process of realizing that I was not leading the life I wanted to lead. I was tired of the alcohol. I missed Joan Trumpauer. I missed Dorie and Joyce Ladner. I missed MacArthur Cotton and the whole group. I missed my special friends in my hometown.

Accelerating that realization was another dream I repeatedly had, which was deeply disturbing (but at least it didn't cause me to scratch at my chest till it bled). In this recurring dream, I was always being chased by drunken white folks. Many times, I would be caught and beaten, but other times I would escape. Each time I escaped, I would find a dark corner and consume the bottle of alcohol that was always sitting there. At some point, Joan Trumpauer would appear before I finished that bottle of Old Taylor. In the dream, I could hear her repeat, "What are you doing?" I was sure she meant, "What are you doing with your life?"

I was not myself. I knew I had to make a change or die when I received the news that Joan, Anne Moody, and several former class-mates at Tougaloo had been viciously beaten by a mob of white high-school kids and others at a sit-in at Woolworth's Department store in Jackson. It had happened on May 23, 1963, and was allowed to go on for two full hours, with the crowd chanting racist slogans and splattering mustard and catsup while beating and kicking the protestors bloody. A former police officer, Bennie Oliver, slugged my former classmate Memphis Norman, dragged him off his stool, and kicked him repeatedly in the face.

Two weeks later, on the eleventh day of June, my mentor Medgar Evers was shot in the back and killed by white supremacist Byron De La Beckwith as Medgar returned home that evening. He was only thirty-seven years old. I was not in the city when it happened, but I certainly felt the sudden trauma of his assassination. Negroes in Jackson rioted in the streets. Dorie was among hundreds arrested for inciting to riot, and she was taken to jail in sanitation trucks the city had converted into paddy wagons. Hundreds of people walked through the streets of Jackson in a funeral procession for Medgar Wiley Evers on June 15, 1963. Having served honorably in World War II, he was buried with full military honors in Arlington National Cemetery.

Now the question remained: What was I going to do? Especially after learning that the court case challenging segregated interstate travel in the South, my own passionate cause, had been settled. Yes, the class action had been denied in federal district court in Mississippi two years earlier. The NAACP had appealed it all the way to the nation's high court, and back again. After the case was denied a second time in Mississippi, it went to the U.S. Court of Appeals for the 5th Circuit, where it was upheld.

Although this counted as a hard-fought, hard-won victory, there was still much work to be done. It was late summer of that fateful year of 1963, when I told everyone that I was returning to Mississippi to get those couple of physical education credit hours from Tougaloo College, since I was only one semester away from graduation.

I left Kansas City on a bus headed for Jackson, Mississippi, painfully aware that if I had done one decent thing, it had been *not* marrying Regina. I had lost the best part of myself to a ravenous depression and the bottle that went along with it, but I was turning the page now and heading back home, where I fully intended to stay.

At Jackson, I boarded the bus for Prentiss, Mississippi. I sat three seats from the front of the bus. I could remember that seat three was my magic bus seat row number when I rode the bus between Tougaloo College and home during my college days. I think that was a crutch I used so I could say I didn't sit in the back of the bus, and at the same time, I did not attract too much attention from the driver of an almost-empty bus. The driver knew the days of Jim Crow were ending. Often, he didn't ask me to move to the back.

Arriving midafternoon on a hot and muggy August Sunday, I had failed to adhere to an important rule of the movement: Always notify someone of your travel plans. Upon arrival at Prentiss, the town was deserted. There was nobody around, just me and my suitcase. I hadn't called home, because I wasn't sure what I wanted to do with my life, and I figured I would surprise my parents as well. Only the police were present near the roadside bus station. I needed to be smart. I approached the officer, and before he could ask my name I said: "Hi, my name is Thomas. Do you know my father Enoch Barnes, who lives in the Lucas community?"

His reply was, "Yes, I know him."

I then asked if he would mind taking me to my father's house out on Highway 84. To my surprise, he agreed to do so without projecting a sense of menace. Of course, there were no black police officers in Prentiss in those days, which is not to imply that a black officer would have been any more or less approachable. I was afraid, traveling on that trip. Getting into the car I remembered an old trick: Drop something on the ground as you get into the car. You then quickly open the car door and retrieve only a part of it. Doing so allows one to leave evidence of being there, as well as to learn exactly where the door handle is, and how it operates. Mercifully, the trip was uneventful.

Home Again

My typical weight was about 140 pounds, but when I returned home I weighed 122 pounds. My mother said, "Boy, what happened to you?" In a little over a year-and-a-half, alcohol and nightlife had nearly killed me before the Klan or the angry mobs could.

The desire to drink was still with me, but at least I had some kind of plan. I was going back to Tougaloo College, finish my degree, and reconnect with my friends who believed as strongly as I did in human rights for all people.

Well, as the saying goes, "If you want to watch God laugh, tell Him your plans." I traveled to Tougaloo, only to learn that Dorie and MacArthur were no longer in school but were serving on the staff of the Student Nonviolent Coordinating Committee. Physically, they could be anywhere. And what of my dear Joan? Was she in Georgia, Washington, D.C., or Virginia? No one knew. Almost everyone who mattered to me—including Medgar Evers—was gone.

It didn't help that I had undergone something of a personality change. I had become antisocial in Kansas City. I'd gone to only one Kansas City Royals baseball game while I lived there, and I hated the huge crowd, hated the height of the bleachers. I even refused to go to church. It got in the way of my drinking. Lucky for me, I never became paranoid, which would have surely put the final nail in my coffin; I would never have been able to escape back home.

Yet, now that I was here, nothing was the same, and that fall semester, something happened to bury any desire I had to finish school at Tougaloo: A cross was burned on the grounds of the campus. Except for Tougaloo's young white chaplain, Ed King, for whom the cross was meant, none of my closest compatriots for the cause were still there, and the core of student activists had become so weakened, I was disillusioned.

I dropped out of school. And decided it was time to go back to church.

9

~~

The Doors of the Church Are Closed

ISN'T IT IRONIC THAT THE KKK would plant a burning cross on the lawn of a young white Methodist minister? I suppose they thought they had just cause, since Ed King had come up with a new strategy for protest against segregation: it became known as Church Visitation. The idea behind Church Visitation was the belief that "good people" could be more readily found in the church than in the general society. Therefore, we might be able to reach the hearts of the Caucasian pastors and their members and make greater headway toward ending segregation.

Calls for support were sent out to ministers from Northern states, because in many cases church policies within a particular religious denomination differed in the North from those in the South. In the northern United States, the Methodist Church was somewhat more open and inclusive of blacks, while in the South, Methodist worship was divided into separate organizations, or conferences, within the church: one for blacks, the other for whites.

Individuals who were not ministers, but who were interested in visiting some of the white churches in the area, were also sought out. Many times, I felt that I would like to worship with my white brothers of the faith; I was raised in the church. However, it quickly became apparent that my white brothers were not interested in worshipping with me.

I was called a communist many times by people in authority at the white churches, as well as many other names that I prefer not to use here. Being accused of trying to disrupt the service just for wanting to worship was very hard for an already disillusioned young man to take. To be put out of church in such a rude manner was shocking to me, even after all the horrible events I had witnessed.

On World Communion Sunday, October 6, 1963, Bette Poole, Ida Hannah, and Julie Zaugg were arrested at Capitol Street Methodist Church in Jackson for attempting to enter that house of worship. These were Tougaloo College students, so despite my disappointment in the school's SNCC activity at that time, there remained some brave foot soldiers who dared to take a stand. There is no doubt that I was damaged and still turning to drink, but that type of demonstration was something I felt I could do. So on January 19, 1964, a group of us—two white ministers named Rolly Kidder, a Chicago-area pastor from the Evangelical United Brethren (E.U.B.), and Rev. Martin Deppe, a Methodist minister from Chicago, and me—visited that same Capitol Street Methodist Church in Jackson for the 11:00 AM service.

As we left the car with our "look-out" person and ascended the church steps, we were approached by three ushers. We introduced ourselves and informed the three that we were interested in worshiping with them. We noticed that a policeman was directing traffic nearby.

One of the three men identified as an usher shook hands with the two white ministers but refused to shake hands with me. The usher asked us to leave the church. We tried negotiating with them to no avail. The usher signaled to the policeman. We had no money to be bailed out of jail; therefore, we wished the ushers Godspeed and left before the policeman reached us at the top of the steps.

My faith in the church was shaken; we decided to visit one of the black Methodist churches that morning instead. They greeted us in the spirit of the Lord. We sat with the choir and participated in the service. There was a better feeling there.

Shortly thereafter, we went to the white Wesley Methodist Church, where they were having their tenth anniversary service. There were seven of us, and Rev. Ed King, Ida Hannah, and their lookout joined us. There were two people standing near the door. One of them disappeared, we thought, to notify the police. The second man began to read the church policy regarding segregation. Then the first man returned and finished reading the church policy statement. The police arrived with sirens, but remained in their cars while speaking with other church officials. The church officials refused to invite us inside to worship.

Later in the evening, our group as well as other groups met at Tougaloo College to assess our activities of the day. These meetings, as well as others that followed, gave all of us the opportunity to give testimony to our true feelings, to search within ourselves for some aspect of racial healing. Also, when bail money was forthcoming, we could put more emphasis on this type of protest.

The church visitation at this time was meant to continue the pressure on the various church denominations to embrace religious integration. Many of my Tougaloo classmates had been arrested, some more than once, while attempting to integrate churches. Marveline Faggett from Dallas, Texas, along with many Methodist ministers from Illinois, were arrested for attempting to worship with my white brothers of Jackson, Mississippi.

Rev. Martin Deppe of Chicago, who was part of the group that

comprised the Capitol Street Methodist Church visitation, com-
posed an article for the *Mississippi Journal*. Dated February 2, 1964,
it related our activities as we engaged in some of those church visitations. The *Journal* retells the experience we shared at the Jackson
churches on Sunday, January 19, 1964. The following is an excerpt
from the *Mississippi Journal*:

A report of a Church Visitation to Jackson, Mississippi, January 18-20, 1964
by Martin Deppe

I would like to share with you something of my experience on a recent weekend visit to Jackson, Mississippi. For a number of months teams of Methodist laymen and clergymen from a number of northern states have traveled to Jackson on a church interracial visitation effort. The story really begins last summer when mixed groups of nearby Tougaloo Southern Christian College students began visiting Jackson churches. The rationale comes from the young white college chaplain, Rev. Edwin King:

I know a little integration in the church isn't going to change a society as sick as Missis-sippi's. But people here respect religion very highly. I figured that if any Negro right would be accepted, it would be the right to worship anywhere. And once integrated contact in the church is established, I have enough faith in the church as a powerful social institution to think the potential for other advancements is tremendous.

A few churches opened their doors, but in most cases the students were turned away. "You can worship here, but not him." The "team" would remain on the steps as a silent witness to parishioners as they entered and later left the service. Suddenly, on October 6, 1963 World Wide Communion Sunday, three girls from Tougaloo were arrested on the steps of Capitol Street Methodist Church. Held incommunicado from noon Sunday until 3 PM. Monday and given one telephone call one hour before going on trial, they were charged with disturbing public worship, fined $1000, and sentenced to six months in jail.

An alert Chicago reporter, Nicholas Von Hoffman, picked up the news off the wire service, noting that two of the girls were from the Chicago area, and gave it a late-edition headline in The Chicago Daily News. A concerned Chicago Methodist telephoned Ed King long distance to ask if there was anything he could do. Rev. King invited him to come to Jackson and stand with the students, which he did the following Sunday. His name: Stanley Hallett, of the

Church Federation of Greater Chicago. He brought the story back to Chicago and the Interracial Council of Methodists (ICM), which accepted the challenge of outside support. The very next Sunday, October 20, four Chicago clergymen, seven Tougaloo students, and one faculty member were arrested. Bail money in the amount of $9500 was reached after almost a week of emergency telephoning among Chicago-area Methodists. And, the Methodist-E.U.B. (Evangelical United Brethren) Freedom Fund was born.

Since October, 1963, teams have come from Wisconsin, Iowa, Detroit, Cleveland, New York, Pittsburgh, as well as Chicago. Concerned E.U.B.'s have joined this witness to support their hope that the E.U.B. Church will face this issue as they discuss merger with the Methodists. Many have been disturbed by the method or approach that is used. Jackson is just one situation; church visitation is just one approach. It may be the wrong approach. But it does attempt to expose a cancer in the Church to the Methodists in Jackson, to all Methodism, to the coming General Conference, to the E.U.B. Church, to ourselves in our own situations. Jackson has become a symbol of our common sin. We can only speak for ourselves, and I knew that I would be going to Jackson.

On January 19, 1964, I went to Capitol Street Methodist Church for the 11 AM service with Rolly Kidder, an E.U.B. seminary student at Naperville, and Tom Armstrong, a Negro student from Tougaloo. Our chauffeur remained in the car as an "observer." Walking up the steps we were met quickly by three ushers (a policeman supposedly directing traffic had moved to the sidewalk a few yards from us and mumbled something into a walkie-talkie).

I began, "We would like to worship with you," and then introduced our group.

The usher gave his name reluctantly, shaking hands with Rolly and me, but not Tom. He said, "You will have to leave. The Official Board has declared this a segregated church. There will be no entrance here by force. I am just carrying out the Board policy."

I replied, "My understanding of the Methodist Church is that it is open to all. Scripture says 'Come unto me, ye who labor and are heavy laden.'"

The usher said, "Well? I don't want to argue. You will have to leave." I asked, "Who is Lord of the Church?"

The usher replied, "God is Lord of the Church, but these people have built this church and they are responsible for it."

Rolly said, "We are simply witnessing to the belief that in Christ there is neither Greek nor Jew, male nor female, slave nor freeman."

The usher shot back (growing

belligerent), "Don't preach to me. I've told you twice to leave and I'll tell you once more." (He motioned to the policeman.)

Rolly said, "We will be going. I hope that you will be free someday." I added, "God bless you."

From Capitol Street we went to a Negro Methodist Church where we were warmly greeted and asked to sit up front in the choir and participate in the service. How at home we felt in an open church!

The major confrontation of the weekend occurred at Wesley Methodist Church at a 3 PM. Tenth Anniversary Service with Bishop Franklin and Dr. Leggett (District Superintendent) in attendance. We arrived as a team of seven, including one Negro student, Ida Hannah, and Chaplain Ed King. The ushers seemed surprised. One usher disappeared to call the police. The Chairman of the Official Board stepped forward, greeted us cordially, and nervously read to us

the policy statement of the Official Board. Halfway through, he stopped, "I can't go on." Another usher finished the reading. (When the police arrived with sirens, two ushers hurried over to the police car to keep them at the car—they obviously wanted no arrests with their own Bishop inside the church.) We answered by reading the statement of the Methodist Council of Bishops made in Detroit last November, one sentence of which reads: "To arrest any person attempting to worship is to us an outrage." They replied that the Bishops' statement was a recommendation only, an ideal. I answered that their Bishop had accepted this recommendation and they were defying their Bishop.

The Board Chairman replied, "The Bishop is our guest here this afternoon." I pleaded, "But he is your Bishop." The Board Chairman responded, "No, he is our guest today."

An usher said, "Let's not

investigate the truth at this hour." A team member asked: "Why won't you face the truth?" Usher: "When, now?" Team member: "Anytime." Usher: "The truth hurts."

Board Chairman: "We don't want to disrupt this service. Your visit will just disrupt us and tear us apart. This is our church. We love it. Now please go. We don't want any trouble—we don't want an arrest here today." Team member: "Would you arrest us at church?" Another usher: "We don't want to."

The police moved in and Ed King, sensing the moment of arrest, said suddenly, "Let us pray." The police were invited to join us, but they turned and disappeared. I led a short prayer and everyone joined in the Lord's Prayer. Some ushers were visibly moved. We left quickly as the police returned.

Confrontation of conscience at the church steps was only one part of our weekend visi-tation effort. Our team spent many hours in interviews with the Negro religious leadership, Bishop Franklin, some of the leading Methodist ministers, some key laymen, and, of course, with Ed King, faculty members, and students at Tougaloo College.

Let me reflect upon some of these conversations. Our church visitation constitutes a great threat to the Southerner and his church. But, it seems to be just one of a number of threats to the Southern culture. One of their greatest fears is the Negro vote. 42% of Mississippi is Negro. One layman told me, "It's a question of who dominates whom. There will always be domination." Today the white dominates and only a token number of Negroes may vote. In Holmes County with a 3–1 Negro population, there are no Negro voters. Arbitrary constitutional exams, threats, locked doors, etc., are used to keep the Negro from voting. In two years of SNCC effort in Greenwood, only 48 Negroes were registered out of 2000.

Another Southern fear that we found very strong is the integration of public schools. They fear race mixing and inter-marriage. Many people we talked to felt that it would take Federal troop intervention before the first public school would comply with Federal orders on school desegregation.

An even greater fear is that of deviation from orthodoxy, nonconformity, speaking out among the white community. Dialogue on the race issue is not tolerated—only monologue.

After the Ole Miss bloodshed last year, the president of a life insurance company appeared on a TV station he owns in Jackson and editorialized quite mildly to the effect that mob violence perhaps was not the way to solve Mississippi's problems. The next day, the board of directors of the insurance

company flatly informed him that he was to make no further statements on the subject if he wished to remain president.

In the past year, 50 professors have left or been forced to leave the University of Mississippi. Of the 28 young Methodist preachers, who last January adopted a mild statement affirming the free pulpit, declaring segregation a sin, saying that the closing of the schools was too great a price to pay, and finally that they were anti-Communists—of these 28, 14 have been forced or pressured out of the state.

The Southerner's greatest fear, I believe, is himself. The nervousness, the tension, the defensiveness that we met suggests this fear. The only humor, the only openness that we encountered over the weekend was not in the white, but in the Negro community.

The Southerner is imprisoned, is in fear of his neighbor, of his whole way of life, of himself.

Bishop Franklin stated to an earlier team, "I may go to Hell for it, but I will not take a stand."

The confrontation of conscience is fearful and painful to the Southerner because it throws into question his whole way of life. Every dealing he has ever had with Negroes will now be exposed. It would make sin of what had been custom. And so, they continue to believe that the Negro is not quite a human being. And, they live with this illusion, because like every person they fear judgment. They live in what one Mississippian calls a "fog of fear." One Negro student at Tougaloo said half jokingly to a white student, "After we get free, we're going to free you."

Why should these threats be so serious, so fearful? Because any one of those threats could establish a crack in the dike. Any one could burst the bubble of their illusion of Southern greatness and the myth of historical persecution. Any one could begin the breakdown of their way of life.

Many of those Mississippi natives paid dearly for their contributions to the quest for equality. Before the cross was burned on Rev. Ed King's lawn on the campus of Tougaloo College, he and his friend John Salter were traveling together in a blue Rambler. They were hit by another car on Hanging Moss Road on June 18, 1963, six days after Medgar Evers's assassination; Medgar was a dear friend to them both. Somehow, Ed King ended up unconscious. The police called the Rambler incident a "traffic accident."

Rev. Ed King also suffered disfiguring damage to the right side of his face when his head smashed into the car's windshield.

But none of that stopped him from championing the Civil Rights Movement. Unfortunately, there was another movement afoot that would cause us to lose many of other other white supporters, due to its militant stance. That movement was known as Black Power.

Black Power

Before the Freedom Rides and all that followed, I had attended a National Student Association (NSA) meeting in Philadelphia. It was in 1960 that I hitched a ride from Tougaloo with three white NSA students from New Orleans. For a good part of the trip, I rested mostly on the floor in the rear of the auto. They were not enthusiastic about the meeting and spoke very little on the way back.

At that 1960 NSA meeting, I encountered my first introduction to the concept of Black Power. I believe that H. Rap Brown was present. I expressed opposition to points set forth by Black Power advocates on the grounds that they would alienate whites in the movement and reduce funding abilities for various projects. Needless to say, my opposition became one of the lone voices crying in the wilderness of nonacceptance. I was shouted down.

In his speech at Berkeley, California, Stokely Carmichael once again promoted the Black Power philosophy. This is surprising to many, because they had the belief that Black Power was not spoken of until after 1964. However, Black Power was a notion of Carmichael and others in the early days.

I believe that later events proved my analysis to be correct. For almost an entire week in 1999, I read the Mississippi Sovereignty Commission file titled "Informants F, X, Y, and Z," which deals mostly with the Mississippi Freedom Democratic Party and various other organizations that were established by dedicated freedom fighters during the middle sixties.

My purpose for the review was to try to gain an overall picture of the time when I was absent from Mississippi. As I anticipated, many whites became disillusioned and left the Student Nonviolent Coordinating Committee (SNCC) and the movement in general. These were good people I had worked with, people who put their lives on the lines many, many times, only to be encouraged to leave the movement to organize the white communities. Most refused to do so and walked away.

I couldn't blame them. I believed with all my heart that both black and white support was needed to make racial progress, and after all the sacrifices they had made, Black Power was pushing these white foot soldiers out the door.

It wouldn't be long before I was ready to join them.

10

≈

Chicago Bound

THERE WAS A LOT GOING ON in that winter of 1964 beyond the Church Visitations that the visionary Rev. Ed King had initiated and promoted. Since I had dropped out of Tougaloo College, I decided to apply to Millsaps, the white Methodist college that had an exchange program with Tougaloo, thanks to the efforts of Dr. Ernst Borinski and the Rev. John Mangrum, who preceded Ed King as chaplain. However, the tolerant views of some of the students and faculty there apparently did not transfer to its institutional practices, at least, not in my experience. Millsaps' denial of my admission was a devastating blow with which I struggled greatly.

Coupled with that event was my attendance at the January 1964 trial of Byron De La Beckwith for the murder of Medgar Evers. I hadn't been in Jackson for Medgar's funeral, but now that I was back in the city, there was no question I was going to make my presence felt in the courtroom, where at least an attempt would be made to see that justice was carried out.

Dorie Ladner, who had been working with SNCC in the Delta, came to Jackson for the trial. She was the first from the band of student activists I had been part of at Tougaloo who I encountered since my return to Mississippi nearly half a year prior.

She was only planning to be in the city for a few days before returning to the Delta. The judge had declared open seating in the federal courtroom. Therefore, we both insisted on sitting in the white section, as we should have been able to do, even as some whites tried to block us from finding space. But De La Beckwith would go to trial for Medgar's murder not once, but twice, in 1964, with both ending in mistrials by all-white juries who couldn't reach a verdict.

Although I was not at the second trial, it was reported that Governor Ross Barnett, whose term ended that same year, interrupted the proceedings to shake hands with De La Beckwith. He did so while Medgar's widow, Myrlie Evers, was testifying.

I guess there came a point where I just couldn't take all the hate and injustice any more, and that point was gathering momentum like a wrecking ball that was poised to swing.

I will be the first to admit that I did not put ample effort into finding my old friends when I first returned to Tougaloo College that fall semester of 1963, and that as it became increasingly clear that my time and options were running out less than a year after my return, I really did regret that. Hard choices had to be made yet again.

After the De La Beckwith trial and my denial of acceptance at Millsaps College, I was as done with Jackson as it apparently was with me. As for moving back to Prentiss, conversations with my parents led to the unhappy fact that it was not the right time for me to set up shop in Jefferson Davis County, Mississippi. Dad believed the Klan had not forgotten me, and he had that on good authority from his Caucasian friend in Silver Creek, whose previous tip had me taking off to Kansas City. I was still dealing with the repercussions of my time there, still doing battle with the bottle I had found borrowed comfort in. I'm not sure how aware or unaware my parents were of this ongoing struggle I was having, but I did my best to hide it from them.

I loved my family, and despite all the damage, all the destruction that had occurred in those pivotal years in the movement, I dearly loved my home state of Mississippi. I did not want to leave in the most desperate kind of way, but besides the warning about the Klan, we got word that some in the White Citizens' Council, of which De La Beckwith had been a member, wanted to hang me from the highest tree they could find.

My father and I had previously discussed the possibility of developing a cattle farm. He owned fifty-plus head of cattle, and it would not have been difficult to add one hundred or more to start with. But the per-pound price for cattle had fallen by half in the past two-and-a-half years. The proposal was off the table.

I also gave thought to teaching at Prentiss Institute, the private black junior college in the area, once I finished my degree. That idea was not inviting to me, so I nixed it; but really, those alternate routes to take were all moot anyway, since my parents were not safe—none of my family was—as long as I was around.

That left me with one option: Get out of town. This time, for good.

Since the writing was scrawled like ugly spray paint on the wall, and time was running out, in a last ditch effort I went in earnest search of MacArthur Cotton before leaving everyone and everything I ever knew and loved behind.

I drove to his hometown of Kosciusko, Mississippi, a little more than 100 miles north of Prentiss. I was so desperate to reconnect that I randomly stopped people on the street and asked if they knew Mac. I stopped at two businesses and inquired, hoping by some crazy chance they could put me in touch. No one knew of a MacArthur Cotton. And as I turned around to make that ride home, which would prove to be the last ride to Prentiss for a number of years to come, all I could think was:

I have no time to investigate, I have no time to investigate . . .

That was interspered with the mantra of:

I need a drink, I need a drink . . .

I was a wreck. I was falling to pieces physically and emotionally when I took a train headed for Chicago the very next day. On the train, I said my mental good-byes to Joyce, Joan, Dorie, and Mac. After crossing the Mason-Dixon Line, I felt amply safe to purchase a drink and get enough alcohol into my churned-up system to fall asleep. When I awakened, the train was pulling into Union Station in Chicago.

I had relatives in Chicago who were willing to help me until I could find a job and support myself. My first stop was at an uncle's home. Three days later, I moved in with a cousin who lived on the west side of Chicago. Contrary to perceptions of the time, many of the residents did try to maintain their properties and provide decent places for their families to live. However, it takes more than that to overcome big-city problems.

My cousin's landlord asked me to work with him as a "fire-escape painter." It didn't take me long to realize that I was afraid of heights. But I desperately needed the job, so I would go to the top of seven- or eight-story buildings and using a paint glove and cans of paint, I would back my way off the top of that building and paint the fire escape from the top until I reached the ground.

Clearly, I was in the wrong profession. As I worked my way down on that last of several buildings, I promised myself that I would never do that again.

The landlord, Roy Mayes, felt sorry for me and allowed me to purchase from him a rusted, three-tone 1955 Chevrolet car for $75. I continued to work for him painting the interiors of homes for two months. After having $25 deducted from my paycheck for three weeks in a row, I had finished paying for the car and had enough left to get a $95 Earl Shibb paint job.

After that, I began working as an assistant manager at a National Tea food store, and from there I went on to work at the United States Postal Service, which provided surprising opportunities to advance the causes closest to my heart, even if I was no longer residing where my heart still belonged. I had only been working for the postal service for sixty days when I was called into the office of the Postmaster of the Chicago Post Office, Henry McGee. Was I about to be fired? He and one of his managers explained to me that they had reviewed my record and noticed my college background. They wanted to know if I would be interested in working with the Postal Street Academy, which was a GED program being implemented by the U.S. Postmaster General to be set up in thirteen cities across the country, with three schools in Chicago.

I accepted the position of science instructor. After being certified by the State of Illinois and spending many weeks in orientation training in Mountaineer, New Mexico, I started to work. The students consisted of young people from many gangs in the city who had either dropped out, or had been kicked out of high school, as well as young people who were not affiliated with any street gangs.

I had no doubt that I could advance their knowledge of science beyond the GED stage, but I wanted to do more than that, so I put together what I called a "Black Science" program for them. I told them that "science was everything and everything was science." I visited their homes and pointed out things that could be corrected with the knowledge of science. Many practicality classes would be based on those visits. Students were always involved in special projects. Often we had to encourage them to go home hours after school had closed.

I knew early on that motivation was the key to their training. Motivation was not a problem. I did a lot of team teaching with the math instructor, James Lowe. We often held classes in the local pool halls or in the parks. My commitment was to motivate these young people to learn. There were many sixteen-hour days.

The school administration arranged with the U. S. Postal Service to allow our students to work three hours daily in the main post office building in downtown Chicago. The students were able to earn a little money to purchase the necessary clothing for school and learn the importance of good work ethics.

Not to the surprise of the math instructor or me, we were able to improve the students' education by two grade levels within a six-month period. We were motivated, and we were good at what we did. There were very few altercations between students. In 1972, a new Postmaster General was appointed. He stated that the postal service was "about delivering the mail and not about education." After four years, the academy was closed, and I went back into the postal service as a transportation specialist.

I married the lovely Jeanette Strong in 1968. We met through a cousin of mine, and in 1973 the first of our two beautiful children, Cynthia, was born. Four years later our second daughter, Kimberly, arrived. Those were the happiest days of my life. I loved coming home to be with them all. We had plenty of fun.

My wife decided that she did not want to be a stay-at-home mom, so she became an office manager at the Illinois Commerce Commission (ICC). The chairman of the ICC was Republican Charles Kocoras. I wondered how that was going to work out. Some years later, ICC Chairman Kocoras was appointed by Democratic President Jimmy Carter to a federal judgeship. He asked Jeanette to be his secretary, and she accepted.

There has never been a better Federal District (Chief) Judge than Judge Kocoras. As for me, I stayed with the U.S. Postal Service and held a number of transportation jobs. The Postal Service paid me well, and I advanced within the system. I retired from the Great Lakes Area Office, U.S. Postal Service on April 2, 2004.

Choices

My wife Jeanette and I often wonder if we were "good parents." We wonder because we can't determine the fail/pass grades. We don't even know if there is such a thing as "pass" or "fail." Therefore we determine parental success by "our" standards.

As far as we know, neither of our children became addicted to drugs, alcohol, or tobacco. They are considered to be good kids. They've both made good and bad choices. We as parents have also made good and bad choices. We don't condemn them for their failures because of ours. We taught and continue to teach them, and try ourselves to learn from our errors and move on.

I did move on after leaving Mississippi. After a period of getting established and raising a family, I started going back to the place of my birth for funerals and to attend to family business, such as maintaining property. For more than I decade, I have been researching my family history. Documenting my ancestors has given me a great source of personal satisfaction.

In 1987, when I went back for Uncle Nemirah's funeral, it became one of those prized, occasional reunions with some of the people with whom I grew up. A group of us guys stayed up late one night talking and someone had a bottle of whiskey, which was shared. I drove back to the nearby home of relatives with whom I was staying and parked in the driveway. It was so late, I didn't want to awaken anyone, and so I slept in the car—until I was jarred awake.

Why in the world would I be approached by a police officer while I was sleeping in a car that was parked in a relative's driveway and get arrested for DUI? I'll never know the answer to that one. I was required to pay a $1,500 bond, and, after that, I never took another drink of alcohol.

Some years after the movement, a cousin, John Branson, spoke to me about my sudden departure in 1964 from our home state. He was much younger than I, and someone who regretted having never participated in the civil rights years. He asked me, in jest, "Why did you allow the Jackson, Mississippi chief of police to run you out of town?"

In trying to honestly answer the question for myself, I thought back to those days of turmoil and inequity and staring death in the face, a far different time when we had no idea of what the outcome might be. . . .

There I was, a young black man who had participated in more voter registration campaigns, sit-ins, pickets, church visits, and marches than ninety-nine percent of Tougaloo College students, suddenly giving it all up. What about my commitment? What about my friends who were left behind? *What happened?*

What I realize in retrospect is that there was not "a" reason that I left; there were ten thousand reasons I left. Yes, there are others who had maybe twelve thousand reasons to leave, but stayed. I suppose it boils down to the basic fact that I left because I wanted to, and I have a tendency to judge myself harshly for that.

I left because of the life I had been forced to live in the state of Mississippi. I left because my father and I had at one time been prepared to take the lives of others before they could take ours. I left because less than thirty-five miles from my house, a young black man, a voter registration organizer, was shot and killed on the courthouse lawn in Brookhaven, Mississippi. I left because of threats to my family. I left because my best friend had been sent to Parchman prison, and I thought that I would be dead before her three months were served. I left because no white man had ever been convicted of killing a black man in Mississippi. And I left because I would have been just another "dead nigger."

Those were hard times. They were dark times of murder and beatings that were sanctioned by the great State of Mississippi. They were times that tried men's souls. And that included the soul of one of "The Little People": Thomas Madison Armstrong III.

There you have it—some of my reasons for leaving. And they don't satisfy me, even though to this day I still believe that in 1964, the end of my life was at hand, and I would not be here now had I stayed.

So, no, Cousin John Branson, I didn't allow the Jackson, Mississippi chief of police to run me out of town.

I left town in order to be able to speak with you today.

11

≈

Reflections

URING THE TIME WE WERE ENGAGED IN the civil rights
movement, no one knew how it would turn out. We were
just trying to end racism, and as far as we knew, it had been such a
formidable force, it could not be stopped by the human sacrifice of
hundreds of thousands of Americans killed fighting the Civil War.
After the tour of struggle over civil rights, which was not unlike
active duty on the front lines of war, many activists, including
myself, returned to our communities withdrawn, introverted, and
depressed, because we felt that freedom had not been achieved.

Most of us were wounded in one way or another from those experiences, but were offered little, if any, support for the well being of our physical and emotional health. Thus, our problems remained unchecked and untreated.

I guess Ivanhoe Donaldson, a field secretary for SNCC, said it best: "I think there was a heavy toll in that generation, on people who were active. It's not to be romantic. I think the evidence is just there. Even today, when you look around for what happened to SNCC people, I mean, some of them are just barely functioning."

The task of being involved in the movement indeed took its toll on many of us. Research by former civil rights workers in the San Francisco Bay Area, who were organizing a national network of movement veterans, found in the year 2000 that workers in rural communities bore the brunt of the tension, and are among those who have experienced most of the problems. Some of us handled it better than others.

If our other partners—whether they were in the movement, on the Freedom Rides, or from the media—were physically beaten, it was internalized as failing to perform our duty successfully. In other words, we didn't influence the chief of police enough to force him to control the mobs. It was on our watch that the mobs harmed our coworkers in the struggle.

The result was post-traumatic stress syndrome at its best. Make no mistake; there are reasons for the stories heard about my fellow civil rights workers who allowed themselves to be overtaken by drugs, alcohol, and other dangerous vices. Clearly, I was not immune to the fall out myself.

Yes, the weighty burden of race, segregation, hatred, and prejudice rested heavily on my shoulders. Yes, I was abused and scorned. And yes, I have wept for those who died for the cause to be free. I can still see the struggles of "The Little People." But it is the memory of what they endured that keeps me grounded, for this I know:

Their struggles were for me.

I believe it is truly tragic that the stories of the "Little People" —the ordinary "foot soldiers" of the civil rights movement—have hardly been told. Although the stories of the great leaders have been presented, efforts of "the least of these" languish in invisibility.

The heroic "foot soldiers" are the individuals who decided that it was time to do something for the Cause. They decided that they had lived all their lives to be free, and now, if necessary, it was time to die for that freedom.

Had you asked any "foot soldiers" if they knew that they might be killed while participating in the next march or sit-in, they would have responded with a resounding YES. Many would have told you they expected to be killed before they returned home from a demonstration. But the foot soldiers realized there was power in numbers, and if their number came up to die, at least they had dedicated their lives to doing all that was humanly possible for a worthy cause. It is due to their efforts that civil equality was won for all Americans.

What amazed me in the early sixties was that very few of my schoolmates were direct participants in the struggle. When I would sit in strategy sessions held in the campus home of Rev. Ed King, I would look around and count the number of people present. Typically, there would be anywhere from twelve to fifteen, and that's out of an entire student body. We didn't fault other students for not being there. We simply said that we had to make things better, and if not us, then whom? What we didn't appreciate at the time, but have a better understanding of now, was that many of our fellow students had parents who were teachers, and their participation could have jeopardized the livelihood of entire families.

Today when I speak with my "friends of the Spirit," we often wonder how it was possible for us to do some of the things we did. We went through some hellish experiences together, which created unbreakable bonds of friendship.

Many of us began under the guidance of Medgar Evers, and one of the things that he instilled in us was that our part in the movement exposed us to risk; that as we did our part in the movement, we must always remember that we could be the next to die. With this in mind, we allowed the man upstairs to chart our course. Wow! What a course He set.

While I knew it would be dangerous to become a civil rights

worker, I didn't know how dangerous. It was not only a war—it was hell. Even now, people sometimes ask me: "What are you doing for the Cause?" Of course, I explain a few small things, such as my participation as a poll worker, but the question hurts, because my mind takes me back to those dark and difficult days, days when black people lived in constant fear of white people. It takes me back to those experiences that I no longer wish to relive. For more than forty years, I refused to share those experiences with anyone. My best friend in the movement was disowned by family members because of her participation in the movement. Some friends in the movement were beaten, and some were shot, while others were tortured in the Mississippi jails.

In more recent years, I have been asked to speak to school groups, and civic and community leaders in the Chicago area, where I continue to live, about my experience in the civil rights movement, particularly regarding the Freedom Rides.

I'm often asked: "Did the civil rights movement achieve all its goals?"

My answer: "No." However, when we decided to take a stand for human rights and against discrimination, we made unheard-of changes to Mississippi's tightly controlled caste system, which had been in effect for more than three hundred years!

We opened up Mississippi's closed society. We opened up Mississippi's closed educational system. We opened up the political process for blacks in Mississippi, which has, in turn, opened doors for other disenfranchised minorities in this great country.

It is through the efforts of the movement that succeeding generations have been able to proceed with new constructions of humanitarian goals. And what should those goals be?

This is a question, that, as responsible citizens, we should never stop asking ourselves. As for me, I do have a dream: All Freedom Riders and friends of Freedom Riders coming together as a virtual unit, using modern technology and promoting particular issues of human rights in the name of the "Freedom Riders."

I envision promoting the "all for one" doctrine for any and all civil rights activists who are in need of economic help and health care.

We should give the interviews; we should teach our youth. We should never let America forget what happened to its children.

Some time ago, a wonderful organization, The African American Leadership Roundtable, Inc., asked: "Where do we go from here?"

I asked them in turn: "How equal is education for the poor as opposed to those who are more affluent?" As minorities, we are no longer barred from the front doors of higher education, yet our dropout rate is the highest of any group. We must change this by making sure our children are provided the best education that we can afford to give them.

I told them most people agree that decent housing is a basic right. Yet millions of Americans live in substandard housing or have no housing at all.

And I told them that they *must* become informed voters. Most of all, make sure that our families are registered to vote. There is no reason that any person, no matter their ethnicity or color, should not be registered to vote.

We must begin to look at our immediate communities and zero in on these three problem areas—education, housing, and the political arena.

Where do we go? I say to you: Go with God. Remember, small things, like the "Little People," can grow into larger things, sometimes far larger than we dare dream.

In the New Testament, it is said that the "sower scatters seeds." Some seeds fall in the pathway and get stomped on, and they don't grow. Some fall on the rocks, and they don't grow. But some seeds fall on fallow ground, and they grow and multiply a thousand-fold.

Who knows where some good little thing that you choose to do will take root, and what result it will bring in the years and generations to come.

Be the sower. Scatter seeds.

Acknowledgments

⧼≈⧽

THIS BOOK WOULD NOT HAVE BEEN possible without the interest and enthusiasm of Michele Matrisciani, Candace Johnson, Larissa Hise Henoch, Lawna Patterson Oldfield, and Robert Solomon at HCI Books, the editing and organizational skill of Olivia Rupprecht, the expertise of our attorney Frank K. Wheaton, and the encouragement of my granddaughter, Aleena. A special thanks to Ellen Freuderheim.

I also depended on the invaluable support and counsel of many friends and family members, especially: Mrs. Nellie Hollins, Mrs. Velma Gamblin, John Branson, each of my siblings, all of my family, the Lucas, Mississippi community, members of the Lucas Tabernacle Church of Christ Holiness, the Tougaloo College family, Rev. Ed and Jeannette King, Mrs. Jessie Armstrong, Mrs. Ernestine Bell and the Rev. Dr. William James, the Meadville, Mississippi native and Godfather of Harlem, New York.

I would be remiss if I didn't acknowledge the mentoring I received from the late, great Medgar Evers, whose courage and documentation of cases of brutality and injustice in Mississippi helped force social and political change in the Deep South, and with a nod to all my Mississippi Freedom (Civil Rights) Movement brothers and sisters: Dorie Ladner, who always brought out the courage in me even when the courage of a country boy was lost; Joan Trumpauer, whose love and spirit transcended even a dream; MacArthur Cotton, on whom many times I leaned, as we walked through the valley of the shadow of evil and death; my dear friend and college classmate Mary Harrison for standing with me during a time of uncertainty and to Jan Hillegas, it was through your effort to put some order to my thoughts that helped make this book possible.

Book Club
Discussion Questions

1. *Autobiography of a Freedom Rider* vividly examines the cultural differences between the North and the South during the 1960s civil rights movement. What examples within the book do the authors provide to illustrate this divide? Does the divide still exist?

2. What does "freedom" mean to you in the context of a democracy?

3. Compare the various tactics used in the strategy of nonviolence employed during the civil rights movement. Do these tactics remain an effective tool of protest in the twenty-first century?

4. Were you aware of the Journey of Reconciliation? Why is it hardly spoken of today?

5. What does the term "foot soldier" mean to you? How can this term be interpreted today? Are there any modern-day foot soldiers? Who do you think they are, and what makes them foot soldiers?

6. In Chapter One, Thomas recounts how, as a child, he knew blacks and whites were treated differently, but he had been

protected from the harsher realities of segregation until he attempted to buy ice cream alone at a Dairy King counter. How do you feel about his reaction? Had you been in his shoes in that place and time, do you think you would have reacted any differently?

7. Chapter Three examines voting inequities and the courage it took to challenge authorities for the right to vote. Do you believe the author's descriptions of his experiences support his opinions about the importance of voter registration? If so, how? What instances or passages are most persuasive to you?

8. Tougaloo College plays a major role in Thomas's civil rights involvement and that of the core of student activists who changed history with their commitment to the civil rights cause. Have you have heard of Tougaloo before? Do you think it is unusual for an historic black institution of higher learning to have a white president, a white chaplain, and faculty members from around the world on campus? What is the name of the reverend who was the target of a cross burning on the Tougaloo College Campus's lawn?

9. In addition to the Freedom Rides, other daring attempts were made to protest segregation in the South, such as interracial group visits to "White Only" church services and sit-ins at

Woolworth's department store lunch counters. Compare the tactics used and the dangers involved.

10. Medgar Evers was a tremendous influence on Thomas and other key individuals in the civil rights movement. Do you believe progress may have occurred more slowly in Mississippi without leaders such as Evers to help guide those young people—or was this a movement whose time had come?

11. Discuss the Freedom Rides and the retaliation against the riders in Alabama and Mississippi. To what degree do you think the Ku Klux Klan, the White Citizens' Council, and the police orchestrated the mob violence against the riders, and were they working together or as separate entities?

12. Black Power conflicted with some philosophies of nonviolence adopted by organizations such as the NAACP. Do you think it influenced the pace of the civil rights movement? Was the movement hurt by division within its ranks caused by philosophical differences, despite the desire to reach common goals?

13. In what ways is Thomas's story most inspiring? Most troubling? What are your own hopes for the future of our country, and what can we learn from its segregated past?

Author Notes

⧼⧽

Introduction

John Dittmer, *Local People: The Struggle in Mississippi for Civil Rights in Mississippi* (Urbana and Chicago: University of Illinois, 1995), 60

"Rosenwald Renovation Project Granted by MS Dept. of Archives and History," Prentiss Headlight (September, 2002)

Mike Miller, *Renewing the Beloved Community: Walking Wounded Project*, concept paper, Bay Area Veterans of the Civil Rights Movement (San Francisco, 2000), 2

Jeremy D. Mayer, *Running on Race: Racial Politics in Presidential Campaigns 1960–2000* (New York: Random House, 2002)

Chapter 1. Opportunity Denied

Richard Powell, *The Blues Aesthetic: Black Culture and Modernism* (Washington, D.C.: Washington Project for the Arts, 1989)

Prentiss Normal and Industrial Institute, "History," *Founders' Day Program*, May 8, 1980

Melerson Guy Dunham, "Message from a Bystander," Prentiss Normal and Industrial Institute, Founders' Day Program, May 8, 1980

Gary Pettus, "The Pride of Prentiss: Graduates Honor 100-Year Legacy," *Clarion-Ledger*, May 6, 2007

Jaman Matthews, "Remembrance of Days Past: The Prentiss Institute at 100," Heifer International Newsletter, 2005-06

Jean Gordon, "Everybody has a Story to Tell: National Oral History Project Collects Conversations (Mabel Middleton and Paul Purdy on Prentiss Institute)," *Clarion-Ledger*, January 17, 2007

Angela Stewart, archivist, Margaret Walker Alexander National Research Center, Jackson State University, Interview on the Subject of Prentiss Institute and Founders Jonas and Bertha Johnson, September 20, 2010

C. James Fleming and C.E. Burckel, eds., *Who's Who in Colored America*, (Yonkers-on-Hudson, New York: C. E. Burckel & Associates 1950)

Kelefa Sannah, "The Wizard: Before There Was a Black American President, Black America Had a President," *The New Yorker*, Feb. 2, 2009

Booker T. Washington, W. Fitzhugh Brundage, Introduction, *Up From Slavery*, (Boston: Bedford/St. MartinPress), 22–27

Phyllis Norwood, e-mail interview on subject of Prentiss Normal and Industrial Institute, July 14, 2010

Neil McMillen, *Dark Journey: Black Mississippians in the Age of Jim Crow* (Urbana and Chicago: University of Illinois Press, 1990), 11–113

Ralph Ginzburg, *100 Years of Lynchings* (Baltimore: Black Classic Press, 1988)

Arthur F. Raper, *The Tragedy of Lynching*, (University of North Carolina Press, 2009)

Aaron Henry with Constance Curry, *Aaron Henry: The Fire Ever Burning* (Jackson: University Press of Mississippi, 2000)

Eric Foner, Manning Marable, eds., *Herbert Aptheker on Race and Democracy: A Reader* (Urbana: University of Illinois, 2006), 158

Susan Klopfer, *Where Rebels Roost: Mississippi Civil Rights Revisited* (Lulu.com, 2005)

Pete Daniel, Eric Foner, eds., *Standing at the Crossroads: Southern Life Since 1900* (New York: Hill and Wang, 1986), 155–165

John Dittmer, *Local People: The Struggle in Mississippi for Civil Rights in Mississippi* (Urbana and Chicago: University of Illinois, 1995), 6–41, 44, 46–54

Myrie Evers-Williams, Manning Marable, eds. *Autobiography of Medgar Evers: A Hero's Life and Legacy Revealed Through His Writings, Letters, and Speeches* (New York: Basic Civitas Books, 2005), 94, 122

H. D. DARBY, on behalf of himself and others similarly situated, Plaintiffs, v. James DANIEL, Circuit Clerk of Jefferson Davis County, Mississippi, and Joe T. Patterson, Attorney General of the State of Mississippi, Defendants. Civil Action No. 2748 in the United States District Court for the Southern District of Mississippi, Jackson Division. November 6, 1958.

Chapter 2. The Environment

Zora Neale Hurston, Carla Kaplan, ed., *Every Tongue Got to Confess: Negro Folk-tales from the Gulf States* (New York: Harper-Collins, 2002)

Lucius Outlaw, *On Race and Philosophy* (New York: Routledge, 1996)

James Brief, *Hometown Mississippi, 3rd edition*, (Town Square Books, 2000)

Joyce Ladner, *The Ties That Bind: Timeless Values for African American Families* (John Wiley & Sons, 1998)

Karl Fleming, *Son of the Rough South: An Uncivil Memoir* (New York: PublicAffairs, 2005)

Chapter 3. Education of the Mississippi Negro

Clarice Campbell, Oscar Rogers, Jr., *Mississippi: The View from Tougaloo* (Jackson: University Press of Mississippi, 1979)

John Dittmer, *Local People: The Struggle in Mississippi for Civil Rights in Mississippi* (Urbana and Chicago: University of Illinois, 1995), 28-30, 86-89

Minion Morrison, *Black Political Mobilization: Leadership, Power and Mass Behavior* (Albany: State University of New York, 1987), 68-69

Jeff Forret, *Race Relations at the Margins: Slaves and Poor Whites in the Antebellum Southern Countryside* (Louisiana State University, 2006)

Mike Miller, *Renewing the Beloved Community: Walking Wounded Project*, concept paper, Bay Area Veterans of the Civil Rights Movement (San Francisco, 2000), 2

Barbara Ransby, *Ella Baker and the Black Freedom Movement* (University of North Carolina Press, 2003)

Chapter 4. Cornerstone: Tougaloo

Chris Asch, *The Senator and the Sharecropper: The Freedom Struggles of James O. Eastland and Fannie Lou Hamer* (New Press, 2008)

Charles Payne, *I've Got the Light of Freedom: The Organizing Tradition and the Mississippi Freedom Struggle* (University Press of California, 1997)

Charles Evers and Andrew Szanton, *Have No Fear: The Charles Evers Story* (Wiley, 1996)

Tom Dent, *Southern Journey: A Return to the Civil Rights Movement* (University of Georgia, 2001)

Chapter 5. Becoming a Freedom Rider

Raymond Arsenault, *Freedom Riders: 1961 and the Struggle for Racial Justice* (New York: Oxford University Press, 2006)

David Halberstam, *The Children*, (New York, Random House, 1998)

Attack dogs trained by Nazi storm trooper
(Mississippi State Sovereignty Commission Record # 2-72-1-104-1-2-1).

Chapter 6. In the Stillness of the Midnight

Mary Hamilton, *Freedom Riders Speak for Themselves*, (pamphlet, 1961)
Posted Sept. 13, 2010 at www.mississippifreedom50th.com/blog

Home of Mrs. Willie Mae Cotton was bombed, McComb, Mississippi
(Mississippi State Sovereignty Commission Record # 9-31-146).

A pawn in this game was Katherine Pleune
   (Mississippi State Sovereignty Commission Record
   # 2-140-3-1-2-1-1 and 2-55-4-65-1-1-1)
Samuel BAILEY, Joseph Broadwater and Burnett L. Jacob, Plaintiffs, v. Joe T. PAT-
   TERSON, Attorney General of the State of Mississippi, The City of Jackson, Mis-
   sissippi, Allen C. Thompson, Mayor, Douglas L. Luckey, Commissioner, Thomas
   B. Marshall, Commissioner, W.D. Rayfield, Chief of Police of the City of Jackson,
   Mississippi, Jackson Municipal Airport Authority, Continental Southern Lines,
   Inc., Southern Greyhound Lines, Illinois Central Railroad, Inc., Jackson City Lines,
   Inc., and Cicero Carr, Defendants. Civ. A. No. 3133, United States District Court
   for the Southern District of Mississippi, Jackson Division. April 7, 1962.

Chapter 7. Friends of the Spirit

Horace Newcomb, professor, University of Texas at Austin, "The Least of These: Ed
   King's Face, Joan Baez, and George Wallace," reflections on Paul Stekler's documen-
   tary *George Wallace: Settin' the Woods on Fire* (March 10, 2000)
Dorie Ladner, Interviews July 18 and 25, 2010
Denise Nicholas, *Freshwater Road* (New York: Pocket Star, 2005)

Chapter 8. Disillusioned

Myrie Evers-Williams, Manning Marable, eds. *Autobiography of Medgar Evers: A Hero's
   Life and Legacy Revealed Through His Writings, Letters, and Speeches* (New York: Basic
   Civitas Books, 2005), 262
Charles March, *The Last Days*
Pat Watters, *Down to Now* (1993)

Chapter 9. The Doors of the Church Are Closed

W. Astor Kirk, *Desegregation of the Methodist Church Polity: Reform Movements That
   Ended Segregation* (Rose-Dog Books, 2005)
John Salter, Hunterbear

Chapter 10. Chicago Bound

Howell Raines, *My Soul is Rested*, (New York: Penguin, 1983)
Mike Miller, *Renewing the Beloved Community: Walking Wounded Project*, concept
   paper, Bay Area Veterans of the Civil Rights Movement (San Francisco, 2000), 2
Peter Jan Honigsberg, *Crossing Border Street*, (Berkeley, California: University of
   California, 2000)

About the Authors

∞

Thomas M. Armstrong is a veteran of the early 1960s civil rights movement in his native Mississippi. He was at the forefront of early protests led by black Southerners for voting rights and equal public accommodations from 1958 to 1961, resulting in threats that had him running for his life. Mr. Armstrong moved to Chicago, where he has resided since 1964. He remains closely allied with other former Freedom Riders and civil rights workers around the country and often speaks at schools and civic organizations such as the African American Leadership Roundtable in Chicago. He has been the subject of scholarly research by respected academics, sought after for major media interviews, and featured in print from critically acclaimed books to a Forbes magazine publication.

Natalie R. Bell is a journalist based in New York. She has worked for more than twenty-five years as a broadcast and print reporter. Her work has been carried by national and international news organizations such as Dow Jones & Co. and National Public Radio. Bell specializes in covering public affairs, particularly those related to education. As a Fulbright-Hayes fellow, she covered political and cultural transition in post-apartheid South Africa. Bell was a delegate to the United Nations World Conference Against Racism in 2001. She has also taught journalism and media studies as an adjunct professor. Bell has family roots in Prentiss, Mississippi, and met Armstrong while researching her family history. She is a native of Nashville, Tennessee, and has lived and worked as a television news reporter in Mississippi.